Rethinking Policy Analysis and Management

Enhancing Policy Development and Management
in the Public Service

Published by: Commonwealth Secretariat,
                 Marlborough House,
                 Pall Mall,
                 London SW1Y 5HX.

Copyright   Commonwealth Secretariat 1999

All Rights Reserved. No part of this publication may be reproduced, stored in a retrieval system, or transmitted in any form or by any means, electronic or mechanical, including photocopying, recording or otherwise, without prior permission of the publisher.

May be purchased from:
Commonwealth Association for Public Administration
(CAPAM)
1075 Bay Street, Suite 402
Toronto
Ontario
CANADA M5S 2B1

Telephone: 1 (416) 920 3337
Facsimile: 1 (416) 920 6574

or from the Commonwealth Secretariat's distributors:
Vale Packaging Ltd
420 Vale Road
Tonbridge
Kent TN9 1TD
Britain

Telephone: +44 (0) 1732 359387
Facsimile: +44 (0) 1732 770620

ISBN: 0 85092 583 5

Price: £9.00/US$14.00

Printed by the University of Toronto Press Inc.

Rethinking Policy Analysis and Management:
Enhancing Policy Development and
Management in the Public Service

Managing the Public Service
Strategies for Improvement Series: No. 8

Commonwealth Secretariat
1999

FOREWORD

A strong and achieving public service is a necessary condition for a competitively successful nation. The Management and Training Services Division of the Commonwealth Secretariat assists member governments to improve the performance of the public service through action-oriented advisory services, policy analysis and training. This assistance is supported by funds from the Commonwealth Fund for Technical Co-operation (CFTC).

Commonwealth co-operation in public administration is facilitated immeasurably by the strong similarities that exist between all Commonwealth countries in relation to the institutional landscape and the underlying principles and values of a neutral public service. In mapping current and emerging best practices in public service management, the Management and Training Services Division has been able to draw on the most determined, experienced and successful practitioners, managers and policy-makers across the Commonwealth. Their experiences are pointing the way to practical strategies for improvement.

The publication series, *Managing the Public Service: Strategies for Improvement*, provides the reader with access to the experiences and the successes of elected and appointed officials from across the Commonwealth.

Rethinking Policy Analysis and Management looks at how the problems of policy analysis and management hinder efficiency and proper implementation; how these problems can be tackled in the light of recent advances in policy development and management science; and how solutions can be found that will ensure that the state improves its role in policy development and policy management.

In searching for answers to these questions, it proposes that a research and development effort be undertaken in order to generate organisational behaviour and the institutionalisation of a new policy process paradigm, and offers a practical framework within which policy can be conceptualised, formulated, implemented and evaluated.

The series complements other MTSD publications, particularly the *Public Service Country Profile* series which provides a country-by-country analysis of current good practices and developments in public service management. Our aim is to provide practical guidance and to encourage critical evaluation. The *Public Service Country Profile* series sets out the where and the what in public service management. With this new Strategies for Improvement series, I believe we are providing the how.

Michael Gillibrand
Acting Director and Special Adviser
Management and Training Services Division

ACKNOWLEDGEMENTS

This publication owes much to a group of permanent secretaries and top officials from the Ministries of Finance and Public Service in the Southern African states that constitute the Southern African Development Community (SADC) who attended the Policy Analysis Workshop held in Harare, Zimbabwe in September 1998. The workshop was designed to assist these senior officials in responding to the rapid changes in and challenges of policy development and management. The formulation and implementation of public policy reform requires thorough and focused training in order to build a capacity to improve the delivery of service to the public and to develop skills and knowledge in policy analysis and management.

The workshop brought together participants who are directly involved in the formulation and implementation of the Economic Structural Adjustment Programmes and in development systems and procedures of implementing the change process in the reorganisation of human and financial resources. The problems of co-operation, consultation and co-ordination between the Ministry of Finance and the Ministry of Public Service were common throughout the region.

The workshop was jointly organised by the Management and Training Services Division of the Commonwealth Secretariat and the Southern African Regional Insitute for Policy Studies (SARIPS) based in Harare.

Very particular thanks are due to Dr. Ibbo Mandaza, Executive Director of SARIPS, and his staff who organised the workshop and provided the essential services that made it a success. Thanks are also due to the resource persons, and in particular, Dr. Mandaza, Mr. Job Mokgoro, the Director General of the North Western Province of South Africa, who provided the necessary guidance and inputs. Mr. Mathias Chakalisa, Deputy Director of the Directorate of Personnel and Management of Botswana, and Mr. Kaluba, Head of the Policy Analysis Unit in the Government of Zambia who provided exemplary models of policy analysis and co-ordination. Thanks are also due to Roy Chalmers and Greg Covington for their assistance in the editing and production of this publication.

The conclusions of the Harare workshop have been broadened by reference to the many other public service seminars and workshops which the Commonwealth Secretariat has facilitated, and through discussions with many senior and top officials and managers in the public service across the Commonwealth with whom we work on a daily basis.

Although in editing, every attempt has been made to retain the accuracy of the contributions, final responsibility for any introduced errors or inaccuracies rests with me. The inclusion of any statement in this publication does not imply that it is an exhaustive analysis of current trends or that it is the official policy of any government.

Sam Agere
Special Adviser
Management and Training Services Division
Commonwealth Secretariat

CONTENTS

Foreword	v
Introduction	1
Purpose and Background History	6
The Political Economy of Public Policy in Post-Colonial Africa	11
Limitations and Constraints in Policy Formulation and Collaboration	14
Methodological Issues and Path to Policy Selection Mechanisms	17
Rationale for Developing a Policy Framework	23
The Framework for Policy Analysis and Management	37
Emerging Issues and Challenges	39
Best Practice Guidelines for Policy Analysis Management Framework	47
Institutionalisation of the Policy Analysis Framework	49
Models of Policy Analysis and Management	55
Botswana	55
Zambia	57
Zimbabwe	65
Towards Regional Policy Co-ordination and Collaboration	69
References	71

PUBLIC SERVICE REFORMS

INTRODUCTION

Increasingly, the global, political, economic and social changes experienced all over the world are having a direct impact on the Commonwealth countries in general and on the Eastern and Southern African countries in particular. Specifically, the impact has been experienced not only on the political processes of establishing or strengthening democratic governments and institutions but also on the economic policies and strategies that have been formulated in the region. The economic structural adjustment programmes which have been implemented in the region are similar in the assumptions, policy, content and purpose, strategy and methodological approach. The strategies, while similar if not the same, have been implemented in different countries with different levels of development. The management strategies which have been instrumental in implementing these broad, similar economic and political processes, philosophies and policies have also been affected, if not reformed to suit the global changes.

There is a realisation that the current globalisation of the market-driven world economy has resulted in the way policies are formulated and managed. The market-driven structural adjustment programmes in the region, for example, have resulted in policy and management strategies of downsizing bureaucracies. The strategies have been seen in some instances as a process of reducing the work-force levels of global enterprise organisations and become leaner and fitter to enhance their competitive advantage in the global market-place. Such managerialist strategies have brought about job lay-offs. The job cuts have negatively affected certain social groups in society and benefited others. The downsizing strategy is a management practice which places the worker at the centre of corporate strategic planning through organisational redesigning and delayering. It can be conceived as a necessary reduction of management layers to realise local responsiveness and accountability and enhance global competitiveness of multinational enterprise. In some countries the strategy is now being implemented without planning or is being treated as given and has therefore become a mindset, the assumptions of which have not been examined by policy analysts. These strategies are a reflection of the intrinsic ways the world economy is structured and how invariably they impinge upon the management systems in the region. An observation has been made which clearly shows that most of the reform strategies have not been subjected to rigorous scrutiny or theoretical examination as to their suitability to the economy and the region. Further, the strategies have not followed the usual format or stages of policy formulation which normally involves many stakeholders. In other words, the process of consulting and co-ordinating with other ministries and departments before the policy is pronounced has not been followed in the current globalisation of the economy and public administration.

The outcomes of some of these strategies are now being experienced a few years after implementation. Because of the nature and type of effects of these outcomes, many policy analysts have been persuaded to question their validity and subject them to theoretical examination.

Globalisation, rapid change and complexity have led to the demand for better services and the pressures for accountability have come with a large dose of uncertainty about the way policy should be formulated and managed. These developments have generated widespread demands for new types of state responses, processes and procedures in the policy analysis.

Many governments are indecisive about the role of the state. Some are torn between pressures for a minimalist role of the state in the social sphere and states involvement in production, distribution and consumption of services. According to the minimalist approach, the state should confine itself to mitigating the temporary maladjustments that occur as the trickle-down effect theory began to work. The minimalist view assumes limited involvement of the state in the economy, preferring the market forces to play a dominant role.

The rethinking or reconstruction of the role of the state has inevitably led to the rethinking and reconstruction of the policy-making paradigms. This entails tackling the following basic questions:

(a) What are the truly strategic policy analysis and management problems that hinder efficiency and implementation of policies?

(b) How can these policy problems be tackled in the light of the advances in policy development and management science?

(c) How can solutions be found that will ultimately ensure that the state improves its role in policy development and policy management?

At the global level, a new policy development and management paradigm is emerging with policy analysis models, tools, hypothesis and technical proposals which are very different from those which predominated for much of the post-colonial state. A transition from administration to management is under way.

The challenge faced by many states in the region is how to accommodate the special problems and characteristics of change in the latest developments in policy analysis, formulation and management. The process does not consist of copying policy analysis tools and methods which are archaic; the challenge is much broader and more complex. It is a matter of seeing whether it is possible to re-examine, rethink and reconstruct policy management approaches, techniques and strategies on the basis of recent innovations in the understanding of the emerging problems. This rethinking of policy analysis and management would be the starting point for designing, on that basis, appropriate technical solutions and approaches. What is being proposed, therefore, is a vast research and development effort, based on experiences, to generate organisational behaviour and the institutionalisation of the new policy process paradigm.

In this context, Rethinking Policy Analysis and Management attempts to answer some of these questions and offer a practical framework within which policy can be conceptualised, formulated, implemented and evaluated. It, therefore, offers a critical review of fundamental questions of the aims, assumptions and effects of the economic reform strategies. In general it attempts to fill in the gaps in the policy development process, which has often omitted the conceptualisation and evaluation stages. For example, it challenges the notion that the determination of government policy is the responsibility of the minister alone within the convention of collective responsibility of the whole government for decisions and actions of every member of it. In determination of policy, a civil servant has no constitutional responsibility, and no role distinct from that of his or her departmental minister[1].

Tradition, therefore, holds that the minister formulates policy and the civil servant implements it. This paper is arguing for a much more broad-based framework which includes the government, civil society, and other stakeholders in all the policy development and management processes.

The need for evaluation of some of these processes is advocated in this paper. This approach is necessitated by the absence of attempts to find out if the objectives of the reform programmes were achieved. If, for example, the purpose of the Civil Service Reform was to improve efficiency and effectiveness of the Civil Service and to ensure its affordability and accessibility over time, then evaluation should focus on the purposes rather than on strategies. Currently, strategies for reform such as downsizing, become the major focus for evaluation. The extent to which the civil service has been reduced and the extent to which public enterprises have been commercialised seemingly become the success measurement factors instead of efficiency and effectiveness as the main purposes for reform. This is obviously a way of measuring wrong goals with the right instruments.

The following main strategies advocated and practised by many countries in the region, have not been subjected to the full processes and stages of policy development and management. The weaknesses and faults in these strategies have contributed to the need to review the framework within which the policy is designed and implemented.

1. *Diagnosis and preparation*

Prior to the formulation of the economic reform policy and to the design of the structural adjustment programme, there was no open debate or consultation with the stakeholders for whom the policy was designed. There was no analysis of the constraints to be faced by the stakeholders in order to draw upon knowledge and experience from the citizens. Diagnostic studies which are participative in process are necessary if a consensus on the problems and the required corrective action are to be achieved. Such an approach would contribute to the development of an action plan to which consumers and stakeholders show their commitment and support.

2. Vision and strategy

Very often, visions of government were not in place at the time that governments implemented the economic structural adjustment programmes. There was, therefore, no link between vision and strategy for solution of economic problems. The overall programme objectives, instead of being driven by the intended outcomes, were based on the need to achieve the effects or aims of the globalisation process. Consequently, the expectations and aspirations of the public were not considered. The role of the state and the nature and type of the civil service desired were never debated and were unknown, leading to the build up of resistance to the reform itself, both by the public and by the civil service which was expected to implement the reforms. In such circumstances the civil service could not have developed the capacity to reform itself. Experience now shows that the civil service reform requires a comprehensive strategy which addresses all the main constraints in an integrated way and sets specific objectives with targets or benchmarks against which progress can be judged. These should be linked to the desired final outcomes such as improved service delivery; meeting the needs of the people; and the size, structure and cost of the civil service. The reform strategy also needs to be realistic and to reflect the available implementation capacity of the service.

3. Sequence and time-frame

The sequencing of the economic reform programme has been haphazard and has always been associated with economic crisis. The time-frame for implementation has not taken into account the availability of financial and human resources, managerial capacity and the degree of support for reform among the stakeholders. In some countries, the economic reforms were imposed while the administrative reforms were in the process of being implemented. In other instances, the restructuring of ministries, reduction of the size of the civil service and improving pay levels were not sequenced in a way which would take into account any interdependencies. In general, downsizing or right-sizing should take place after ministerial reviews because these will identify redundant posts and personnel to be retrenched. In some countries, pay reforms have been implemented before retrenchment of staff resulting in resistance for administrative reforms in which citizens have become suspicious of government intentions.

4. Process approach

In most of the reforms, there has been no meaningful participation by stakeholders. Greater use of participatory techniques such as workshops and team-based project preparation methodologies have not been used in many countries of the region before the reform is implemented. Process approach generally requires that the stakeholders adopt a flexible approach to project design so that programmes can be adopted and changed in response to evolving circumstances. Such a participative approach has often not been encouraged at the initial stages of policy design.

5. *Strengthening of core functions*

In developing civil service reform interventions many governments did not take necessary measures to strengthen their core functions in order to improve resource mobilisation and allocation, policy making capacity and the effectiveness of the state machinery. The strength of these processes depends upon training of civil servants and improving their morale. Strengthening of core functions should take place across the entire civil service while at the same time taking into account sector-specific management and policy needs.

6. *Capacity building*

The reform programmes have been designed and implemented without regard to the local capacity to execute the programmes. Training policy and programmes that help to develop skills and build capacity in areas related to civil service reforms, were not in place at the initial stages. There has been little support for training managers in the civil service and policy analysis in order to improve performance and productivity. Attention was not given to gender issues to ensure that equal opportunities were promoted and that the impact of redundancy, redeployment and credit facilities would not be adverse. Social dimensions of adjustment programmes were always considered as an afterthought. They were therefore not built in when the programme was conceptualised, thereby revealing a weakness in the current policy analysis framework.

The weaknesses and strengths of the way in which the civil service reforms were introduced and implemented can now be studied by the students of policy analysis and management. In the main, the reforms were hurriedly prepared and implemented, usually following an economic crisis, without regard to the need to involve stakeholders in formulation and evaluation of the policy intervention strategies. The academic institutions such as the Universities that have the resources to provide advice by way of policy studies, were never involved nor utilised. In some instances where institutions were created by government with a specific purpose of providing advisory services, situated in either departments or in the office of the Head of State and therefore employed by government are not utilised and their advice is not taken seriously[2] In other countries, such policy analysis units have been reduced to taking Cabinet minutes or memorandum, which is contrary to their employment conditions as well as to their skills and knowledge.

Amongst some of the problems experienced in managing the reform programmes are the lack of co-ordination and co-operation between and among ministries. The lack of co-operation and consultation signifies the absence of an institutional mechanism which can resolve the problems, being experienced. Among the service delivery systems, there have been no specific studies of delivery standards and the level of involvement, utilisation and access to public service by some social groups in society, for example, women and the poorest of the poor. Such surveys would help to improve both the design of the civil service reform and the monitoring of its impact. Repeat surveys should be made in order to identify the need to take any corrective measures to mitigate any adverse consequences.

The lack of a policy evaluation process is exacerbated by the lack of policy dialogue, on the civil service reform, with relevant organisations, social groups and individuals. The lack of a dialogue, using consultative group or Round Table process, is a reflection of the protection of interests by the dominating social group in society and state.

PURPOSE AND BACKGROUND HISTORY

The purpose of this publication is multifold. In general it is based first on experiences of managing conferences, seminars and workshops on policy formulation, management and evaluation throughout Commonwealth countries. Secondly, it arises from the policy advisory services provided to member states by the Secretariat in which strengths and weaknesses of policy management have been observed. Thirdly it is based on the views, observations, and comments made by senior and top officials who attended a regional workshop in Harare in September 1997 on Policy Analysis. Among these many purposes are:

1. **To attempt to provide a theoretical explanation on why, how, and what policies are conceptualised, formulated, implemented and evaluated. It also explains the rationale of either accepting or rejecting policy options.**

    While policies have a political and administrative content, they have a political base since they constitute a problem-solving mechanism and conflict resolution instrument in the distribution of power and resources. At the base of all the public policies are power relations. The political economy theory is therefore an attempt to understand the way resources are produced, distributed, allocated, consumed and managed in order to achieve a particular goal within society. The theory also explains the relationship between the countries of the region and the world economy which has been undergoing fundamental structural changes. It assists the politicians, policy advisers, senior servants and those who direct public service, who approach policy and strategy formulation and its implementation in a variety of ways. It also provides a broad view of the socio-economic and political environment from which policies are formulated and managed.

2. **To improve the seemingly purely narrow technical or institutional approach to the policy management process particularly in the reform of the civil service.**

In the past, little attention has been given to the policy process by researchers, practitioners and or the donor community. Most government institutions responsible for research are either unfamiliar with the policy process concept or are uncomfortable with it. This publication should contribute to the study on policy process, particularly the identification of boundaries, demarcation of its essential peculiar features and identification of dynamic elements and the extraneous forces which impact on it. Unless serious attention is given to policy analysis and evaluation, the efforts of enhancing policy management may not be effective. Thus, an efficient and effective policy management process is essential, if not a prerequisite, to sustainable economic and social development.

It is argued that the organisational structure, management systems, technical skills, knowledge, information system, and overall infrastructure must be available and of a high quality to be able to understand the intricacies of policy development and management. In many countries of the region such capacities are absent, hence their inability to successfully manage the reform of the public service. The experiences of the several civil service reforms carried out by many countries in the region in the Seventies and Eighties should have warned these governments of the dangers inherent in the externally-determined reforms, often imposed, and the likelihood of their failure. Nevertheless, either because of the absence of a historical memory within African governments, or because of the poor means of sharing information and experience or because of the weakness of the governments in the face of pressures from international financial institutions, the civil service reforms which were identical were accepted and implemented during the last ten years using the same philosophy and practices.

Reforms were expected to be implemented by a civil service whose organisational culture was archaic and therefore could not sustain any changes with which it was not familiar and which often threatened its existence. This publication therefore aims to assist bureaucracies to appreciate the need to place emphasis on policy analysis and management, paying particular attention to the conceptualisation and evaluation of the policy processes. It is important for policy managers to realise that the policy management process encompasses a much wider arena than the civil service, though it is central part of it. The multiple links with government on the one hand and civil society on the other, can be properly established through studies, debates and regional sharing of experiences.

3. **To support quantitative and qualitative research and evaluative measures on whether or not the goals of the administrative reforms are being achieved.**

   In this regard, measurement indicators are suggested, the theoretical perspectives are recommended and the socio-economic and political environment within which the reforms take place are discussed. Such discussions will widen the horizon, limitations and strengths of the administrative systems in managing the policy process. The study also fills the gaps in knowledge on what constitutes a policy process, since both policy-makers and managers appear to be more concerned with minute details of policies themselves rather than the policy process itself in a given environment.

   It is argued that there is a need to link the objectives of the reform with the results. For example, if the reform was to achieve efficiency and to improve service delivery, the policy analysis studies should be able to assist in the re-focusing or re-assessment of the policy in order to address the problem appropriately.

   Evidence from the reform of the civil service in Ghana, for example, now shows that downsizing and improved pay do not bring about major changes in performance and the delivery of service to the people. Indeed, observers believe that in Guinea, the country with the largest staffing reductions and pay improvements, moonlighting, rent-seeking, and absenteeism in the civil service have not been significantly curbed.[3]

   These problems could be identified through policy evaluation which should be an on-going exercise and should be shared within the region by member states.

4. **To demonstrate, through three case studies from Botswana, Zambia and Zimbabwe, that the administrative reforms can clearly be understood and appreciated if different institutional mechanisms are designed to facilitate the policy analysis and management process.**

   The studies demonstrate this in different ways. First, the link between the state and civil society in policy formulation and evaluation, through a consultative forum. The second demonstrates the need to set up a Policy Analysis Unit which assists cabinet in making the well-informed policy decisions which must be implemented by all ministries in a properly co-ordinated manner. Thirdly, the co-ordination of policy formulation by the policy managers, i.e. permanent secretaries under the Chairmanship of the Cabinet Secretary, and the link between ministers and civil servants.

The studies demonstrate that there are many ways of doing things differently in order to achieve the desired results. These different approaches constitute the focus of the rethinking of policy analysis and management which has been made necessary by the following events, pressures and fundamental changes taking place in society:

1. Once policy development was the unique preserve of the public service, now it is less so. A number of key players in the formulation and management of policy have come on board, e.g. external consultants and international organisation, business community, academics and civil society. The bureaucratic culture which is predicated upon a shared set of values and goals and a centralised and a hierarchical decision-making system have been reformed. Further, there is a formal departure from formulating and managing the policy based on purely traditional, legal, rational and normative construction of public policy.

2. The needs, demands and aspirations of the consumers of public policy and civil society have also changed and require different modes of intervention. Citizens are demanding not just the quantity but also the quality of service delivery making it necessary for the development of new ways of meeting them. Further, the policy management structures and systems are now, more than ever before, expected to be accountable, accessible and answerable to a wider public. Many more checks and balances on the distribution and management of resources have been introduced.

3. Global changes are now globally similar and shared all over the world. The collapse of command control economies, collapse of welfare statism in developed countries and growing difficulties faced by dependent economies and former colonies, for example, have all had an impact on policy changes in many countries. The strategies for downsizing or right-sizing the public service and decentralising the functions of government have all had an effect on the way in which policies are formulated.

4. The decrease in the amount of resources available, the reduction in direct control, the increase in the number of players in the policy process and the focus on results have made it necessary to rethink, redesign and reassess the traditional methods of policy development, implementation and evaluation. The need to equip civil servants with skills, knowledge, technology and appropriate attitudes have resulted in changing the way policies have been formulated and managed, in the past.

5. The recognition that "business as usual" no longer applies to today's economic environment and that the organisations need to be fundamentally altered in order to regain or sustain competitive momentum. The need to employ human resources who are proactive in

improving performance have all made it necessary to think differently about the role of significant others in policy-making process. The issues such as empowerment and service standards have affected public service accountability and ethics.

6. Rethinking policy analysis and management has emerged out of the changes in the policy paradigm, new policy planning framework, and implementation of new policy strategies which have clearly shown the roles of each of the players in consultation and co-ordination of policy. It has the active ingredients of good policy such as analysis; political sensitivity; policy and stakeholder analysis; language; symbols; values; communications; approval processes; leadership; creativity; timing, and especially judgement, can be combined for success.

In order to understand the impact of these changes, pressures and imperatives, it is necessary to provide a theoritical perspective of the nature and type of the state that implements these reforms. The philosophical assumptions of the state machinery constitute a base upon which methods and rationale for policy choices are formulated. They help to explain why certain policies are preferred to others at any one particular point in time.

The path that is taken in the policy selection process contributes significantly to the development of a rationale for a policy analysis and management framework. An explanation is given on what constitutes the framework out of which guidelines for institutionalising it are suggested and recommended.

THE POLITICAL ECONOMY OF PUBLIC POLICY IN POST-COLONIAL AFRICA

The subject of public policy is discussed in the context of current national, regional and global challenges. Hitherto, the dominant tendency in such discussions has been to abstract public policy reform issues, divorcing them from the historical, political and economic context of the countries under investigation and according them absolute and universal values and norms. In a world so bifurcated between developed and developing, between globalising *northern hemisphere* and a globalised *southern hemisphere*, both the concept of public policy and the context of reform require deeper scrutiny if they are to be relevant and assist in the current discourse about the future of Southern Africa in particular and Africa in general.

BROAD DEFINITIONS AND CONSIDERATIONS OF POLICY IN THE PUBLIC SECTOR CONTEXT

Public policy is largely a political and social process in the context of the state which, in turn, might therefore be viewed as a public policy arena itself. In this regard, policy is a reflection of a given set of power relations in a given context, period or epoch. At best, a (good) policy is the outcome of the (good) relationship between the state (or those who govern) on the one hand and civil society (or those who are governed) on the other. At worst, a (bad) policy is the reflection of the (bad) relationship between the state and civil society, in which case, such policy might be viewed as no more than an imposition on the part of the (dominant or strong) state over the (dominated and weak) subjects. Therefore, the policy direction in a particular sector or given situation is invariably an expression of the dominant interests in the society.

As a concept, public policy is also an ideological construct, representing the attempt by the ruling class to mask the reality of class relations and disguise the dominant role of the state. Therefore, public policy is no more than the justification – i.e. the ideology – of a ruling class in a given situation such as that which might be termed a *policy* specifically, a policy framework, or, generally as might be represented by the government or regime of the day.

The nature and context of the state is that which necessarily determines the quality and direction of public policy. A strong state is one which is not oppressive and dictatorial; it is one which draws its strength from the confidence reposed in it by the civil society as a whole, and, as such, is responsive to the public will, accountable and transparent.

PUBLIC POLICY AND REFORM IN THE CONTEXT OF GLOBALISATION

Globalisation, liberalisation and privatisation constitute the three core elements of the economic reforms of the newly-emerging global economies. Describing the comprehensive nature of the recent wave of globalisation, Recardo Petrella, provides an insight into the different dimensions of the globalisation process. He writes, "the principal characteristics of globalisation consist of the following:

- the globalisation of financial markets;
- the internationalisation of corporate strategies, in particular their commitment to competition as a source of wealth creation;
- the diffusion of technology and related research and development and knowledge worldwide;
- the transformation of consumption patterns into cultural products with worldwide consumer markets;
- the internationalisation of the regulatory capabilities of the national societies into a global political economic system;
- the diminished role of national governments in designing the rules for global governance.[4]

Arising out of this definition are many analytical and policy questions that can be addressed in the context of its impact on the African region. In particular, the diminished role of national governments in designing rules for global governance indicates the limitations of developing countries in formulating public policies that can solve their unique problems. Consequently, they are always in conflict with the principles of globalisation in the process of addressing their unique problems.

Many studies on globalisation are now revealing its negative consequences. Panchamukhi has shown that globalisation has resulted in increasing disparities between developed and developing world, deterioration in the terms of trade, development of new forms of protectionism by the developed world, and more importantly the frustration of policy autonomy by the developing world.[5] The lack of policy autonomy is demonstrated by the imposition of many of the structural adjustment programmes in the African region with concomitant consequences on governance and public administrative systems.

As pointed out in another work[6], it is, therefore, important to view the post-colonial state in terms of both the *external* and *internal* dimensions. The *external* dimension refers to the complex relationship of historical, political, socio-economic and even cultural factors that are an integral component of the *post-colonial state*. The *internal* dimension refers to the *post-colonial state* itself, within a given geographical or territorial location, the class composition thereof, and the relationship between it and the post-colonial society in general. Clearly, the concept of *post-colonial state* raises important questions about the nature of the relationship between the *external* and *internal*. Suffice it to state that the external takes precedence in that it is first and foremost an integral component of the post-colonial state, and therefore, necessarily and inevitably influences and pervades even the dynamics of the *internal*. The *internal* is not organic, neither in its origins nor in its dynamics; at least that is inevitably so in this historical conjuncture, whether we call this *neo-colonialism*, the era of the dominance of international capital, or relentless *globalisation*.

LIMITATIONS AND CONSTRAINTS TO POLICY FORMULATION, CO-ORDINATION AND COLLABORATION

The relationship between the political economy of the post-colonial state as outlined above on the one hand, and the capacity for policy initiative, co-ordination and collaboration on the other, becomes quite obvious. To begin with, there is the problem of the limited parameters of policy initiative that is inherent in the nature of a dependent state which has its reference the promptings and pervasive influence of metropolitan powers and the various international financial institutions, particularly in this era of intensified globalisation. This is quite apart from the problem of insufficient knowledge and skills for the policy formulation exercise. But even where such skills have been known to be in abundance, as is the case in a number of the older public services in Africa, these historical and political limitations continue to play havoc with the policy world of the average post-colonial state.

Therefore, it does appear imperative that public service training in Africa takes into account the need to expose the policy-maker to the world of political economy through which to develop a capacity to both understand and confront the social reality in which the policy-maker and functionality is operating. In the meantime, both the nature of the post-colonial state itself and the current effects of globalisation will continue to impact negatively on the possibilities of overcoming the related problems of policy co-ordination and collaboration. Needless to add, the best level of co-ordination and collaboration within any government is always based on a *national consensus* about both the causes of the problems to be addressed and, therefore, the means towards their resolution. That this is lacking in most post-colonial states is hardly surprising in the context of what has already been stated before. This is often compounded by the tension between those political considerations that are considered imperative for the survival of the state on the one hand, and the issues of functionality and effective government on the other. For example, the size of government about which conventional wisdom emphasises "downsizing" in the interests of both economy and efficiency. In the African context, however, the number of ministries is often dictated by such political considerations as are related to the need to build the broadest *national coalition* as part of *nation-building* and promoting *national unity*. But this in turn renders difficult – and sometimes impossible – the need to "downsize" or "right-size" the public service. Yet *size* is an important factor in co-ordination and collaboration: the larger the government, the more difficult to co-ordinate; and the more serious the problem of collaboration in a situation within which factionalism becomes the order of the day and decreasing financial resources make it increasingly difficult to effect functional consensus among the key factors in the government.

In turn, the impact of the structural adjustment programmes and accompanying public service reform measures have so far helped more to exarcebate these problems than ameliorate them. This is particularly so with respect to the need for retrenchment and the inevitable loss of some of the most able civil servants, the declining attraction of public service salaries and conditions of service, and the erosion of public confidence in the public service in particular and government in general. Therefore, not only are public services confronted with the problem of declining capacity and legitimacy; even governments are now threatened at their very core.

However, there is also tension between two major categories of public policy, reflecting also the traditional dichotomy that has developed over the years with respect to the state's ability to perform quite badly in one while doing better in the other. This is the tension between the *macro-economic* policy framework in which, as stated earlier, the post-colonial state lacks the wherewithal to conduct an autonomous strategy that would break the historical and economic constraints already established during the colonial (and neo-colonial) era. On the other, there is the *social* policy area which is so close, central and visible to the majority of the people and therefore one in which any government worth its salt has to be seen to deliver the "fruits of independence", in the form of education, health delivery, housing, labour and gender matters, justice administration, local government issues, etc.

All these constitute not only the cutting edge in politics but also become the most vulnerable as the economic crisis deepens. On the one hand, *social policy* represents the means whereby the state hopes to address the *social deficit* caused by colonialism and under-development. On the other hand, it is what causes the *budget deficit* and thereby exposes the inherent vulnerability of the economy as the country is forced to borrow from international financial institutions, enters into structural adjustments programmes and is caught in the debt trap. As always, there is the accompanying requirement for reducing the budget deficit, mostly on the basis of reduction in expenditure in the *social development sphere*. In turn, this undermines earlier successes in this field and enhances the crisis in education, health and social services delivery in general. The social crisis that ensues expresses itself in the form of the decline of the human resources development programme, and the erosion of human and technical capacity to save the society from the developing economic and political crisis.

These are the roots of the *African crisis* as we know it today: an historical legacy that is inherently self-inhibiting for the post-colonial state; a colonial-type economy based essentially on the export of raw materials and the import of finished products, with the consequent of such economic activities as industrialisation that would increase job opportunities and wealth, while also contributing to the scientific and technological development of the society; the problem of continuity of the economic, political and social structures as opposed to a growing capacity for effective transition through *transformation*; and therefore, a post-colonial state which increasingly finds itself unable to attend to the economic and social demands of the society.

This is the society in which the state becomes increasingly alienated from civil society, is incapable of good governance and is threatened with the loss of legitimacy.

Even *public policy* becomes hollow in terms of both its ideological and functional import. So even previously live and central issues as those pertaining to macro-economic and social policy areas become as marginal to the people as those in the category of defence, security and foreign affairs.

The post-colonial state has clearly certain political, economic and social limitation in developing its own policies which are not entirely influenced by the external forces. However, despite these limitations, the post-colonial state must still deal with issues of power relations, resolutions of conflict, formulate policies and manage programmes and above all deal with the development of its own human resources. The state, in its own way, must resolve problems of social inequalities in society.

Despite the socio-economic and political limitations imposed by the imperatives of the political economy framework, the post-colonial state must be responsible for identifying areas needing state intervention, for example in the collection of revenue, regulating local market forces and take decisions in the process of governing the country. The social policies, for example, health, education, housing, social security etc are decided by the state through its own system and organisational structures.

The post-colonial state, therefore, has the responsibility and decision-making powers in the allocation, distribution and consumption of resources in accordance with its own criteria and principles. Further, it has the capacity and power to adjust its policies to suit the needs of the society. It is, therefore, in this context that policy analysis, development and policy management that the responsibilities of the post-colonial state that the rethinking and restructuring have to take place in order to suit the profound changes taking place in society. The demands for changes, whether from external or internal forces, must be addressed by the state in an organised fashion following certain agreed principles and guidelines.

METHODOLOGICAL ISSUES AND PATH TO POLICY SELECTION MECHANISMS

The selection process of policy intervention strategies and the methodology that is used in collecting information and identifying target groups are closely associated with the ideology of the state and its apparatus. This ideology is generally reflected in the philosophy of the ruling political party through its policy intentions, as expressed by the needs of the social group or class that the party purportedly represents.

The choice of one policy intervention from among many options is premised on the ideology of the party, social reality, historical past and existing concrete conditions. The path to the selection of options, when analysed, can primarily be divided into two levels, namely the negative and the positive.

1.   NEGATIVE SELECTION MECHANISMS

By negative selection we mean that mode of intervention that systematically excludes those strategies that conflict with the class nature of society. This negative intervention takes place through structural selective mechanisms, ideological mechanisms, decision-making mechanisms and repressive coercion mechanism.[7]

What form does each of these mechanisms take in order to be identified as part of a negative selection process? Navarro describes these mechanism as follows:

Structural selective mechanisms: These mechanisms refer to the exclusion of alternatives that threaten the capitalist systems, an exclusion that is inherent in the nature of the capitalist state.[8] The nature of the state could be socialist, post-colonial or nationalist. A post-colonial state, for example, could exclude alternative policies that threaten its existence. The constitutionally guaranteed right to private property, which excludes state conflict with that right and with the class nature that right determines. In Zimbabwe, South Africa and Namibia land and private property rights are constitutionally guaranteed. Any changes to that right such as the redistribution of land, would threaten landowners and their class across the racial and gender divide. In particular, those who inherited the land from their forefathers would feel intensely threatened.

The overall priority given to the property and capital accumulation explains why, when the needs of the people are in conflict with property rights, the latter usually takes priority over the former. Further when health, for example, is in conflict with property right such as land, it is the property that has the priority over other rights. The poor health of farm-workers has always been in conflict with the right to property of the large commercial farmers. Such a conflict is exhibited when farmworkers suffer from malnutrition because they do not have enough land from which to produce nutritious food and the landowner would rather hold on to his land than redistribute it. Another example is the appalling lack of adequate legislation protecting the workers in most post-colonial societies, contrasting most dramatically with the large array of laws protecting private property and its owners. Such patterns of protecting private property are clearly demonstrated in many other institutions such as mines, oil fields and industry. The structural negative selective mechanism also appears in the implied assumption that all programmes and reforms have to take place within the set of class relations prevalent in society.

- *Ideological mechanisms*: These mechanisms ensure the exclusion from the realm of debate of ideologies that conflict with the system. The discussion on the selection of leadership or its succession in many post-colonial, one-party states is always excluded from the realm of debate in the party thus ruling out leadership contesting. However, any debate about a possible successor will jeopardise the would-be successors who can also become the subject of attack by the current leadership because of their threat to the status quo. Such action suppresses any legitimate challenges to the status quo because of the fear of the negative consequences of such contest. All contenders to leadership are therefore eliminated before the selection process begins. The exclusion of ideologies, rules and procedures which question or threaten the basic assumptions of the leadership system is the most prevalent mechanism of the party, and indeed state intervention.

- *Decision-making mechanisms*: The decision-making processes are heavily weighted in favour of certain social groups and classes, and thus against others. The mechanisms, for example, for the selection and appointment of Chief Executives of Public Enterprises, Board Members and Commissions are conducive to the dominance over those bodies of individuals of corporate and middle classes, to the detriment of members of the peasant and lower working classes. The individuals who are generally critical of the state and its apparatus are never appointed to the Board of Public Enterprises or to other important positions of influence. It is equally true that some very competent persons are not selected to serve on Commissions of Public Service because they have progressive ideas or because they support the opposition party and are therefore regarded as enemies. There is usually very little distinction made between political opposition and enemy, as a result, politics and policy measures are not clearly differentiated. This negative culture is inculcated into the mainstream of the ruling party and state machinery.

- *Repressive and coercion mechanisms*: The final form of negative selection, repressive and coercion mechanisms, takes place either through the use of direct force or more importantly, by cutting and thus nullifying those programmes that may conflict with the sources of power within the state organism. The prevention of debate on women's demands for ownership, or joint-ownership between husband and wife, of land in the communal areas in Zimbabwe can be regarded as a threat to the patriarchally-dominated society. Women were therefore denied the same right as men in the drive towards an improved land tenure system in the communal areas.

The abolition of the Ministry of Community Development and Women's Affairs is yet another example in which the state reduced the power of influence of its own machinery. Women's representation and presence, through a ministry, has therefore been effectively downgraded and eclipsed within the overall national machinery of government.

2. POSITIVE SELECTION MECHANISMS

Positive selection refers to the type of state intervention that generates, stimulates and determines a positive response favourable to overall capital accumulation, as opposed to a negative selection which excludes anti-capitalist possibilities. There are two types of such intervention: the allocative and the productive. In the allocative intervention, the state regulates and co-ordinates the allocation of resources that have already been produced, while in the latter, the state becomes directly involved in the production of goods and services.[9]

- *Allocative intervention policies*: These policies are based on the authority of the state in influencing, guiding and even directing the main activities of society, including the most important one – capital accumulation. The policies are put into effect primarily, although not exclusively, through laws that make certain behaviour mandatory and through regulations that make certain claims legal.[10] Within the health services, there are laws or rules that make it mandatory for doctors to register certain contagious diseases such as AIDS/HIV with the State Health Department and for the employers to install protective devices to prevent industrial accidents.

- *Productive intervention policies*: As has been indicated, productive intervention policies are those whereby the state directly participates in the production of resources, for example, medical education, production of drugs in nationalised industries, management of hospitals, critical strategic industries such as steel industry and military hardware industry. The list also includes public enterprises such as telecommunications, broadcasting, electricity and water utilities etc.

Most allocative decisions are administered by the state apparatus mainly the civil service or the administrative branch of the executive, while productive functions take place outside the administrative bodies of the state machinery.

As stated before, the primary role of state intervention is to strengthen and stimulate the economy so that the allocative, productive and distribution policies are maintained and adequately administered. The characteristics of the process of capital accumulation are dictated by the social groups of that state. The primary characteristic of capital accumulation is its concentration. Increased concentration of capital is likely to result in a concentration of labour with its consequential demands for specialisation that fragments the process of production and distribution. Specialisation demands great involvement and investment from the state in order to guarantee the reproduction of labour needed for the system. In the health sector, for example, the state allocates and produces the human resources (doctors and nurses) needed for the delivery of health care, and increases specialisation of labour necessary to sustain the growing concentration of that sector. The same process takes place in the fields of education, housing, transportation and social services.

There is an increased economic concentration. The increased concentration of capital also leads to the concentration of resources in urban areas and deployment of resources to those areas, required and needed for the realisation of capital. The process of urbanisation necessitates a growth in the allocative functions of the state (e.g. land use legislation and city planning) and of productive functions (e.g. roads and sanitation) so as to support, guide and direct that process in a way that is responsive to the needs of capital accumulation.[11]

From this discussion, it appears that the state plays a critically important role in the allocative, productive and distributive policies in the economic development process. The policies, as has been demonstrated, can be based on an ideological perspective of a class that is in control of the state. It is equally true that the analytical methodologies from which policy options are selected, are related to the interests of the state which in turn is composed of and serves the interests of a class that dominates the state. It is therefore argued, through this analysis, that comprehensive public policies are not all that ideologically-neutral nor value-free. Clearly, where policies appear to serve the interests of other social groups other than those in power, it is assumed that they are meant indirectly to facilitate the strengthening of the social group that composes the state. Ultimately, it is the interests of the state that are paramount. Such policies are favoured if they result in peace, stability and maintenance of status quo.

The discussion has contributed to the methodological issues, the path to the policy selection process, the role of a dominant social group in power relations, and the nature and type of problem to be resolved. These all contribute or are related to the assumptions and characteristics of an appropriate and analytical policy framework which is composed of the following critical factors and requisites:

1. The formation of an appropriate policy framework is dictated by the nature and type of a problem that has to be solved, the issues and concerns to be addressed and the general intentions of the state regarding the type of a

society it wants to construct and a civil service it wants to build. The policy formulated in this manner and for these reasons, is therefore issue-based, problem-focused and problem-solving.

2. Such a policy has a particular purpose and by its nature is closely associated with decisions pertaining to the production and distribution of the human, financial and technological resources available in order to resolve a problem or address an issue which is of concern to the public. In this regard, it is goal-directed in order to maintain a desirable type of society required by the state, in circumstances in which external interests prevail.

3. There are many different key actors that contribute to the development of a policy framework. There are formal and informal actors who participate in different ways in the policy formulation. The formal and informal actors may also be internal and external, and their influences depend on their multifarious social and political interests prevailing at a particular point in time. The policy may therefore be externally determined.

4. The actors, types of policy decisions and problems are linked to management and organisation in the process of implementation. In general, management and organisation are designed by the state or a social group that is in power in such a way that the objectives can be achieved. While the organisation is a creature of the state, it may develop its own style, culture, ethos, norms and standards which are necessary for the efficient provision of resources and/or solutions of problems. The organisation has to develop key competencies which are a prerequisite to the effective management or resources for the realisation of the state's objectives. The policy process is dominated by the civil service.

5. The above policy implementation strategies have an ideological base and bias in their assumptions and methodology. This assertion is based on the assumption that any policy decision formulated by politicians, state or ruling social group has a political bias. The bias may be positive or negative to certain other social groups in society and is based on their need either to promote or to defend their interest which may be a threat to them or the status quo and continuity. To this extent, many policies are not ideologically-neutral nor value-free as they are formulated from alternative courses of action and choices. It is assumed that ideology and values influence choices in a number of policy areas such as education, health, housing etc. The provision of free education and health services depends upon a choice being made and being influenced by a particular philosophy or belief system such as fairness, justice, equal opportunities and affordability. Policy is culture-oriented and is influenced by the availability of appropriate resources.

6. All the above issues and factors in policy development take place within a socio-economic and political environment that is undergoing serious and

fundamental changes in governance and economic transformation. The move from military dictatorships, one-party states, socialist ideology and controlled economies to multi-party elections and liberalised economies would require a dynamic policy framework within which objectives are clearly defined and parameters appropriately designed as a way of maintaining and sustaining the direction of change process.

The way forward is essentially to involve stakeholders in the policy formulation process, reforming antiquated management cultures, linking elected officials (politicians) and appointed officials (civil servants) in policy development and above all training, and learning from past mistakes or sharing information with others who have been involved in the same policy process before, such as in regional workshops.

RATIONALE FOR DEVELOPING A POLICY ANALYSIS FRAMEWORK

The way policy intervention strategy is formulated and implemented is a reflection of the nature of the state, its class nature and composition, its main interests, points of strength and weaknesses. While there are certain political and economic limitations to the state's role of formulating an appropriate policy, there are equally some policy areas in which it has strength to develop and implement a strategic policy based on its capacity. By far the strongest policy instrument the post-colonial state has is its human and natural resources. It must be pointed out that its strength can also be the source of its weakness in cases where there are influential external forces that can manipulate the local policy development processes and procedures.

The strengths and weaknesses of a post-colonial state are illustrated by the way it manages its own economy and public service reforms in response to globalisation and by the manner in which it addresses issues of declining performance and productivity by its own human resources and state machineries such as ministers and public enterprises. We will discuss these issues and/or problems and relate them to the way in which reform policies have been conceptualised, resulting in the adoption of particular recommendations, the explanations of which are sometimes not clearly understood. It will be argued that the option taken by government is a reflection of either its weakness or limitation and strength. The examples will also indicate the reasons why certain governments have preferred one option as opposed to another and the mode of intervention without consulting stockholders.

(a) Globalisation and management of the economy

The process of globalisation, as already explained, has political, economic and social factors and forces which influence or sometimes dictate the co-ordination and directions under which change should occur. Globalisation as a process fundamentally assumes the emergence or strengthening of the market economy in the belief, rightly or wrongly, that the private sector is the engine for development.

The changing role of the state with the interested assumption that the government should be small, lean and should have a minimal role in development is another assumption. A case is usually made for a minimalist state, the extent of which is not normally explained or questioned but accepted as given. Critics of this assumption have posed the question of the degree or size of the desired minimalist state, i.e. should the state control 33% or 43% of the economy? The other assumption regarding the role of the state is that it should reduce its welfare programmes and adopt a more regulatory approach, leaving the market forces to operate with the minimum of state influence. This results inevitably in the change of the philosophy of government, i.e.:

- a meaningful and effective response to the demands, needs and aspirations of the people. In this regard the state is expected to create a conducive environment in which the private sector plays a leading role in the development process. However, the demand generally connotes the dictation of the private sector interests. In its response to the needs of the private sector and civil society, the state is expected to be transparent as it attempts to deliver the services, thus promoting good governance and public accountability;

- structural changes are expected to be made in the economy in order to facilitate and promote the private enterprise. In many cases, increased trading is encouraged in order to allow more flow of external capital and the promotion of partnership with other organisations in the developed world. The increase in the flow of external capital is by far the most powerful instrument in influencing governments policies.

The structural changes in the economy according to this paradigm are meant to:

- achieve fiscal monetary discipline, reduce budget deficit, balance budget, remove subsidies, control money supply and inflation;

- achieve trade discipline through the removal of quantitative control quotas, free imports, free exports, providing direct incentives, no trade deficit etc.;

- achieve exchange rate discipline, remove black market in foreign exchange, devalue currency etc.;

- achieve industrial discipline, privatise public sector, strengthen private and financial sectors. Encourage investment, technology and management at home, reform the civil service and improve government/industry interface.

The key reforms advocated are managerialism, commercialisation, deregulation, corporatisation and privatisation. The bureaucracy has become the focal point for change seeking to achieve cost-effectiveness in all that it does; with the argument that traditional values such as job security are no longer affordable in a world dominated by chronic budget deficits and worrying public debts and asserting, as an act of faith, that anything the public sector does the private sector can do cheaper and better.[12]

These changes are supposed to be supported and strengthened by the changes in the legal and administrative systems. As a result of these changes, laws are made to protect property rights, e.g. land and buildings, and individual rights such as recourse to take the government to court in cases of breach of contract.

The changes have an impact on the restructuring of the state machinery, principally the public service. The restructuring is based on the assumption that the civil/public service is too big and is duplicative of other functions of the state. Consequently, according to this assumption, the size of the service must be reduced through various strategies such as redundancies; delayering (removing unnecessary administrative levels); decentralisation or devolution or de-concentration of powers and responsibilities from the centre; deregulation; and above all debureaucratisation.

In all these instances, there has been no research or study conducted to identify the nature of the problem. There is also an absence of thorough consideration given to the appropriateness of the proposed solutions to the identified problems. In essence, there is a lack of empirical evidence about the problems and their solutions. It would appear, therefore, that most of all these assertions are based on assumptions which have never been subjected to a rigorous scrutiny and verification. The problem is exacerbated by the fact that the normal processes and procedures of formulating policy are never pursued in the design of a new policy in order to address an emerging problem or issue.

(b) Problems of performance and productivity

The second problem area in which the nature of the state is identified is the way the issues of productivity and performance are addressed. The way the state handles performance management issues is a reflection of its commitment, will and direction. It also shows its weakness in dealing with issues and problems in which it has powers, despite the limitations imposed by the post-colonial state. The point to be emphasised here is that issues of efficiency and effectiveness of the state are just as important to a socialist or a capitalist state. However, variations are observed in the implementation process.

Since independence, many administrative, managerial and technical problems have been observed but very little has been done about them. While in some respects, questions of performance of the civil service have been studied through Commissions and other relevant internal organisations, the solutions have not been given serious attention. This raises questions about the effectiveness of the existing policy framework, if at all there is one. The following problems and policy issues have been identified:

- There has been a decline in performance since independence. Many commissions have been appointed to look into the decline of performance and recommendations have been made. It has taken some countries ten to twenty years to implement such recommendations. You may want to compare the speed with which structural adjustment programmes have been implemented, and sometimes given a time-frame of five years, for example.

- The technological and knowledge base of management and administration has declined despite the increase in the number of qualified university graduates with skills and expertise to not only maintain continuity but also, and more importantly, to manage the complex reforms that are introduced in an environment which is not ready for the fundamental changes. The problem of the lack of human resources with suitable skills and expertise is exacerbated by the absence of the audit of skills and occupation before complex reforms are implemented. Some countries realised that they did not have the capacity to downsize or right-size the civil service after recommendations were in the implementation process. As a result, it took a long time to implement such reforms. In still other instances, the government relied very heavily on foreign consultants who had little knowledge of the local situation. It can be argued that most of the consultants came from the donor countries that recommended the economic reforms.

- Political interference in the appointment, promotion and discipline of civil service has been on the increase since gaining independence. In some countries, ethnic considerations have an overwhelming influence on appointments of civil servants to senior positions as well as to public enterprises in which government has a stake. One of the consequences of such political interference is that staff are appointed to inappropriate positions or may not have the right level of competence. This eventually affects the quality of performance of the individual and the delivery of services to the people.

The neutrality and objectivity of the civil service is certainly compromised in circumstances in which political considerations outweigh objective and professional criteria.

- Corruption is also on the increase, both among politicians and civil servants. In situations in which there are no checks and balances, corruption has negatively affected the delivery of service to those who need it most. However, some countries have appointed anti-corruption agencies, the ombudsman etc. in order to reduce the level of corruption. One of the aggravating factors in this regard is that corrupt officials are appointed to anti-corruption agencies, thus making it impossible to solve the problem. It should be mentioned that once corruption is institutionalised it is very difficult to eliminate it because it becomes a culture of the organisation and individuals working in them and is therefore deeply rooted in the administrative system.

- The independence of the Public Service Commissions or Civil Service Boards has been curtailed by many governments. Such independence of the Commission has been undermined through various measures such as making it purely advisory instead of being executive. The result is that people are wrongly appointed or promoted or transferred and can therefore be highly misplaced even if they have appropriate qualifications.

- Management systems have broken down. Records and information systems may not be in the right place and therefore cannot be retrieved easily. In some countries, records have disappeared with the result that no decisions can be made. Some police officers are known to lose police dockets making it impossible to bring the culprits before the court and leading to miscarriages of justice. Performance appraisal systems have also broken down. Neither the supervisors nor the supervisees can be assessed for their performance at the end of the year. If the instruments for measuring performance are not in place, to what extent can we talk about achieving the goals of the state efficiently and effectively?

In those countries where the performance appraisals are still in place, the rating of performance by supervisors has become questionable. Most officers, for example, are rated the same. If everybody is rated average, it would be difficult to identify the high fliers and the poor performers. In still other circumstances, both the poor performers and the high-flyers are awarded similar rates of annual increments and bonuses. The morale of the civil servants is consequently affected, with the result that there is a decline in productivity.

- Among the most serious factors affecting good performance is the decline in standards and values of the civil service. Standards and values underpin the whole system of service delivery to consumers. The values of integrity, honesty, dependability, helpfulness, impartiality, courteous, fairness, consistency, efficiency and effectiveness are gradually disappearing from among the civil servants. This is made worse by the absence of any formal system that can reinforce such values. The disciplinary measures have equally been weakened to the extent that nobody wants to take responsibility as this brings many enemies, particularly in small states where everybody knows one other.

The breakdown in the management systems is further complicated by the way in which the budgets are administered for each ministry or department. In some countries, ministries run out of their votes of expenditure six months before the end of the financial year and some civil servants cannot do their work because there is no travelling subsistence allowance. In some extreme circumstances, there are no drugs in hospitals or clinics, no chalk in schools, and no equipment with which to deliver services, such as fertiliser and seed to farmers.

In all the above instances, the government has to take the full blame without apportioning it to external forces. The government has the power to allocate and distribute resources efficiently and equitably since it is in control of its own resources through its budgetary system and human resources that it employs.

The problems of performance and productivity constitute a weak capacity in policy analysis research, development and the management of the existing policies. The weakness in policy analysis and review contributes to the deterioration in the total performance of the civil service with the result that goals are not achieved and public service not delivered. Poor policy management leads to inefficiency and ineffectiveness of the public service machinery as this will be demonstrated in the case studies in this publication. Such problems reveal the absence of an effective policy framework within the state.

However, in Financial Management, policy analysis and development planning contributes to the budget cycle. This is possible when there exists a structured and formal relationship between the institutions involved in development planning and those involved in budgeting. This enables government to do the following:

- link policies, spending and monitoring;
- define sectoral goals, objectives, programmes and outputs;
- restructure expenditure within and between sectors in line with clearly identified priorities;
- provide a rational approach to resource allocation by identifying focus areas which will receive adequate funding and provide value for money;
- determine how policy decisions affect resource allocation and to assess the effects of future budget allocations;
- assess budget proposals in relation to key development strategies.

(c) The characteristics, form and type of reform

Many countries in the Commonwealth are implementing the economic and administrative reforms of one type or another. The implementation of these reforms exhibits peculiar features and characteristics that reflect on the nature of the state. The tactics and strategies that are used are a symptom of the strength and weakness of the state, reflect the dominance of external influence and in some cases show that the state is in control of its own resources. In analysing these reforms it is possible to differentiate between those countries that show a heavy dominance of external forces and those that determine their own policies. It also clearly distinguishes the countries that have been responsible in formulating their own policies from those in which policies for reform are imposed from external sources. The purpose of the reform, the strategies and instruments used, the pace and costs of the reform vary in accordance with the ownership of policy formulation, political will and commitment and the extent to which they control their own resources and are therefore not dependent on metropolitan countries. For the purpose of our analysis, comparisons are made between those countries whose reform programmes were dominated by economic considerations (A group) from those that put emphasis on human resources (B group).

Purpose of Reform

A	B
Reduction of budget deficit and liberalisation of trade. Removal of controls. Encourage private enterprise. Privatise public enterprise. Achieve fiscal and monetary discipline, removal of subsidies. Elimination of black market. Less government.	Improve service delivery. Make services affordable, acceptable and available. Prompt responsiveness to the needs of the people. Better government.

Emphasis, Type and Characteristics of Reform

A	B
Costs reduction Downsize civil service Commercialisation programme Privatisation programme Deregulation Decentralisation	Human Resources Development Performance Management Systems Clarity of goals for reform Develop Citizens Charter Improve morale of Civil Servants Improve Delivery Systems Customer care

Assumptions of two Philosophies/Methodologies

A Supply Side	B Demand Side
Quantitative Statistical Control direction Structural Conditionality Time limit Externally-determined Profit-making	Qualitative People centred Process/Ownership Management Home-grown Own pace Internally-determined Improved knowledge and skills base Evaluation programmes

Instruments used

A	B
Budget control Redundancy schemes Accounting Instructions Joint Ventures/Partnership Legislation Directives Hierarchical structure	Performance Appraisals Systems Performance agreements Training Policy & Career Planning Reward Systems Develop code of conduct Procedures manual Records and Information Management Systems Improve conditions of civil servants

Behaviour Patterns for Manager (P/S)

A	B
impersonal distant inaccessible plan organise control administrator apex of pyramid master/directing	user-friendly proximity accessible communicative consultative participative leader/manager base of pyramid servant of people

In analysing the characteristics, purpose and assumptions of the economic and administrative reforms, it is possible to differentiate between those countries that own and control the reforms and those that do not. Another distinction is related to the origin, initiative or source of the reforms and whether it is externally or internally determined. The emphasis on certain characteristics of the reform is also a clear indication of the present and dominance of external forces.

Taking into account all these distinctions, it would be safe to generalise and make the following conclusion:

1. Most African countries south of the Sahara, with the exception of Botswana, have had their reforms initiated from external sources, and or are sometimes imposed. There is a heavy concentration on economic and financial reforms with less attention being paid to human resources management. According to this observation they are categorised in the

'A' group in which human resources management is considered as an afterthought or as a consequence of the financial and economic reforms but not as a priority. The type of reform imposes the choice of instruments to be used in the reform process, methodologies and the behavioural pattern of those who manage the reform.

2. In the region, Botswana stands out as one country that has initiated, owned and implemented reforms at its own pace without much external pressure. It has placed emphasis on the development and management of human resources while at the same time efficiently managing the economy. It has regarded the reform as a process of change and not as an event which is given a time-frame and other conditionalities.

Within the Commonwealth and outside the Southern African region, Malaysia and Singapore have placed a lot of emphasis on human resources while at the same time efficiently managing the economy. These two countries designed their own reforms and determined on their own the time-frame within which reforms have to be implemented. Essentially, they own the reform process.

3. In most developed countries of the Commonwealth such as Australia, Britain, Canada and New Zealand, due emphasis has simultaneously been placed on both the financial and human resources. The reforms have been determined and initiated from within rather than without. The reforms have been seen as a necessary process of change and are owned by the countries themselves.

(d) The evaluation studies on adjustment programmes

Considering the importance of these policy initiatives on Structural Adjustment Programmes, the impact they have on the lives of the citizens and the financial and social costs to the country, it is surprising to note that very few studies have been conducted to determine whether or not they achieve the desired results. Both the countries that have implemented the economic reforms as well as the donors that have recommended or imposed the conditionalities for reform, have not committed human and financial resources to evaluate the impact of the reforms since this should be an on-going exercise before further changes are made and funds committed for an extension of the programme.

Despite this seeming lack of commitment for evaluation of these fundamental economic and administrative programmes, a few studies have been conducted by the United Nations Development Programme, the European Centre for Development Policy Management[13] and Public Policy at the University of Birmingahm,[14] have revealed the following weaknesses which demonstrate the lack of interest by the state in the use of the available policy framework:

- The envisaged costs savings on downsizing the civil service fell far short of expectations. In some cases, the costs escalated thereby leaving the major problem unresolved.

- There was an absence of institutional provision for co-operation between the two major ministries responsible for reform, i.e. the Ministry of Finance and the Ministry of the Public Service. In still other instances, the Ministry of Finance reached an agreement with the International Financial Institutions without the knowledge of, or consultation with, the ministry responsible for personnel, even in matters of redundancy and administrative reforms. There was great emphasis on saving financial costs at the expense of human costs.

- The reform process was very much dependent on top-down direction and external stimuli. In some countries, the external forces dominated the form of change which was not well understood by those who were to implement the reform programme. The absence of a team approach in managing the reform left a vacuum in which the donor could effectively influence the pace and direction of the change process.

- There was an absence of a training policy which would facilitate and equip the human resources with adequate skills and knowledge to implement a new programme which had never been experienced before and in which they did not participate in formulating. The budget for reform did not include training. In the few instances where training was mentioned in the policy reform document, it was not made relevant to meeting the needs of the civil servants, management and those who were to supervise the change process. It was assumed that once policy was formulated the civil servants would simply obey the instructions and implement the policy whether they understood it or not. This is a traditional approach to policy development which is incapable of meeting the current demands and needs of highly politicised people.

- The management development training institutions were not involved in the policy formulation and were equally ignored in both the implementation of the programme and in training the service in preparation for such a fundamental and structural change in society.

- The reduction of costs and size of the civil service alone did not result in the automatic achievement of efficiency, effectiveness, responsiveness and increase in productivity. Consequently, the reduced civil service and budgetary allocations did not improve the delivery of services such as health, education, agriculture and overall performance in administration. With reduced budgetary allocations, the agricultural extension services were severely curtailed as there was limited allocation for staff to travel to deliver the relevant agricultural inputs necessary to increase food production. The same can be said about teachers, nurses, etc.

- The structural adjustment programme envisaged to make savings from cut costing measures. The savings were expected to be ploughed back into the system to improve the wages for civil servants. However, the new systems of incentives and employee motivation were not consolidated into the reform as adjustment conditions and budgetary restrictions constrain improvement in salaries/wages and incentives. Since there were no savings, some countries proceeded to freeze the salaries of the civil servants, thereby reducing their morale and performance. This was done without negotiation or consultation. One of the consequences of such a freeze in wages was the strained relationship between the state and the Public Service Staff Association. This often resulted in strikes or other forms of industrial action being taken by the loyal civil service. Further, the staff association in their negotiations with the state on wage increases, did not use the costs savings as a criterion but rather the increase in the cost of living and the devaluation of the currency which resulted in the decline of their purchasing power.

- Economic and administrative reforms were introduced at a time when there was a noticeable decline in the performance of the civil service and when the weak capacities of the state administrative capacities had been observed. Various commissions which had been set up to improve performance of the civil service, prior to the economic reforms, had indicated many weaknesses of the different ministries in the delivery of service to the people. Critics of the reform programme have wondered why the state would expect a weak administrative system to implement very complex and fundamental reforms in which it did not have the capacity, know-how and commitment.

- The environment of political instability, social unrest, political interference in the civil service administration, economic mismanagement and highly institutionalised corruption, largely contributed to a degeneration of the entire public service system. Such a system could not be expected to reform itself with success.

- The weaknesses and ineffectiveness of the policy implementation on structural adjustment programmes in many countries of the sub-region reveal the lack of appropriate approaches and strategies to policy development and management. They also demonstrate the lack of involvement of stakeholders, the absence of thorough studies on the nature of the problem to be addressed by the policy measures, the absence of capacity to manage the policy and, above all, the lack of skills in the policy management process. In more general terms, the policy measures have lacked ownership of the policy by the state, thereby giving an impression that the policies were imposed by external forces and that the countries were desperate in accepting the conditionalities of assistance from donors. The conditionalities have exhibited an ideological bias and are exactly identical[15] whether in a small or a large state or in a poor or rich country, giving rise to the belief that they emanate from one source even if the countries themselves claim that such policies are home-grown.[16]

- The lack of understanding of the implications of the policy by policy-makers. The lack of skills and experience in designing policies of such magnitude and the absence of precedents from which to learn and share experiences demonstrate the need to examine some policy models that have been effective in other countries or in other sectors of the economy. The emerging best practices in policy management are also drawn from the most experienced and successful policy-makers and managers within Commonwealth countries which have the same public service corporate culture.

The implementation of the structural adjustment programmes in the region has demonstrated at least four key issues and problems that are experienced in policy development and management. These were also identified by top and senior officials who attended a regional workshop in Kenya in May 1997. The issues were that:

1. African policy-makers do not seem to understand or appreciate their policy environments and the kinds of problems they generate. This is attributed to the social distance between the policy-makers and the rest of the population.

2. Policy-makers seem to be making choices without adequate information because of the poor articulation of differences between political and administrative roles in the policy process. Often politicians would like to seize the initiative in making certain policies and tend to do so without adequate knowledge of the consequences, a problem that could have been avoided if they had listened to experts.

3. The inability to mobilise adequate resources and the inability to effectively utilise available capacity, render policy-making a symbol exercise. Many interest groups are not always aware of the content of the policy until the implementation process begins.

4. The policy evaluation mechanism is sometimes deliberately weakened. Policy-makers in the region appear not to like to hear that their policies are performing poorly. Hence, previous mistakes remain undetected and uncorrected. At the same time, no meaningful lessons can be learnt from past experience within this milieu.[17]

The policy development and management processes often address major problems at the expense of signs and symptoms which include:

- increasing poverty in the midst of natural and human resources;

- varying levels of state integration;

- increasing levels of economic, social and technological under-development;

- abdication of strategic policy analysis and policy-making to external agents such as the international financial institutions, donors and international development agencies;

- short-term v long-term view of events – reactive (for crisis) v proactive policy stance;

- institutional decline as evidenced by:

    (a) inability to attract and retain skilled personnel in the civil service;

    (b) inability to generate, store and disseminate information about the civil service itself, the economy and society;

    (c) inability to respond adequately to challenges from the environment, e.g. new economic blocks, globalisation effects etc.

From this discussion it would appear that there is a need for the development of an effective framework for policy development and management capable of analysing problems, formulation of intervention strategies and evaluation of policy outcomes and impact. The framework that is developed should be institutionalised and strengthened within the state machinery such as cabinet, legislature, ministries and departments and other agencies of government such as public enterprises and local governments.

The policy framework which focuses on the public sector is an important instrument that facilitates the analysis of the problem or issue to be addressed and identifies key issues and practices that should be considered when developing and managing a policy. It also should assist in improving decision-making at all levels in government and should provide an evaluation mechanism which is result-oriented and which provides a feedback on the efficiency, effectiveness and performance of public policies and can be critical to policy improvement and innovation. In essence, it contributes to accountable government.

The evaluation aspect of the framework is an analytical assessment addressing the results of the public policies, organisations and programmes that emphasise reliability and usefulness of the findings. Its role is to reduce uncertainty and improve information flow and gathering. Its main objective is to improve decision-making, resource allocation and accountability, through informing the public, informing key decision-making processes and encouraging on-going organisational learning. Consequently, evaluation forms an important part of a wider performance management framework. A successful framework is one that is based on collaboration between key participants such as consumers of public policy and other relevant stakeholders.

A framework should be credible and have the capacity and capability of being used by interested parties. To this extent it should not show bias or any preference to a particular social group in society and should not be subjected to manipulation or control by any one person since it addresses the needs of society.

It should be mentioned that frameworks vary from one country to the other and depend very much on the political, economic and social conditions which often interact in complex and unforeseen ways in any one country.

THE FRAMEWORK FOR POLICY ANALYSIS AND MANAGEMENT

PURPOSE OF POLICY ANALYSIS FRAMEWORK

While, in the past, the formulation and management of policy has been the sole prerogative of the state and its apparatus, there is now an increasing and growing demand for a shift to a new paradigm which encapsulates the involvement of consumers, public and civil society. Conceptually, the trend is certainly not smooth and has no precedent recognisable by the state machineries. The purposes of the inclusion of significant others in both policy development and management, have as their base, the need to promote good governance and sustain democracy. It is assumed that this incremental trend is a challenge to the bureaucratic tradition of the growth of the state, the modalities of public policy formulation and the tradition of allocation of scarce resources in order to achieve the public good which constitutes part of the economic and social transformation of society. In addition, this trend contributes to peace, stability and development of a national agenda in consensus-building in policy development. Such a policy initiative requires a policy framework within which issues and problems are conceptualised and addressed through an appropriate methodology.

The following are some of the purposes for developing a policy framework within a particular development paradigm:

- To analyse the nature and typology of the problem, the number of people affected, the time-frame and the causal social and political factors. Such an analysis facilitates the understanding of the causative factors of a particular problem experienced by a specific group of people. It also helps to determine the method of intervention which must have the capacity to solve the problem.

- The need and desire to find an appropriate solution to the problem that has been identified. In this regard, the target group or community must also be identified. At the same time, alternative courses of action and policy options must, of necessity, be explored to enable policy-makers to formulate appropriate choices and their impact on other social groups.

- The policy framework provides a rationale for intervention in an environment in which problems are being or likely to be experienced. It further provides the potential and capacity to meet the unanticipated and recurrence of problems.

- It provides the legal and regulatory framework within which policy intervention is necessary without waiting for the legislature to pass a new law each time a problem is identified. It gives the direction, guidelines and procedures which have a capacity of addressing a problem should it emerge in similar circumstances requiring similar strategic actions.

- It assists the state machinery of the implementing agency in sourcing funding to support the action-oriented strategies aimed at solving a problem. Further, it enables the management to control the expenditure of funds. It should be mentioned that the lack of attention to policy framework may well result in shortages of required resources or an under-estimation of complexity of the policy measures.

- Policy framework contributes to the preparedness of the administration in solving conflicts and contradiction in society and assists in developing meaningful ways of addressing the issues, concerns and constraints.

- The arbitration of competing and conflicting groups, individuals and institutions, either in the provision or in the receipt of services such as health, education, housing and social justice in industrial relations. Such institutions may be competing for the same resources or markets and may be unable to find an amicable solution of their own.

- It explains approved and normal linkages with the external environment through a memorandum of understanding, joint collaboration and commissions in certain areas of policy such as in industry, commerce and finance, including relations with international organisations.

- To provide an attitudinal and behavioural pattern appropriate for the implementation and management of a programme or project. The behaviour of institutions and agents of change should be clearly stated so as to inform the public about what to expect from those who provide and deliver services. It therefore contributes to the creation of an organisational culture appropriate for the allocation, distribution and consumption of services.

- The framework also provides certain competencies expected of the officials and organisations involved in the process of policy implementation, a code of conduct for the providers of service, and procedures manuals which give guidance on the delivery of service.

EMERGING ISSUES AND CHALLENGES

The development of policy, in many ways, arises out of the necessity to address the issues and problems arising from the inevitable changes that are currently taking place within the political and economic development agenda. The agenda for development itself suggests that appropriate and meaningful ways be determined in response to the challenges and changes, some of which have no precedents, and which would serve as reference points. Corkery states that "Current development thinking suggests that policy framework is critical in determining the performance of firms, farmers' households, public sector bodies and other economic units. By extension, therefore, the economic development of a country depends on the quality of this policy framework, decisions taken and the processes involved in formulating each decision".[18] The development of public policy assumes in some respects, that the performance of public organisation and state machinery, in particular, be measured and made publicly accountable to the public they serve and from whom they derive their legitimacy and authority.

The achievement of objectives by public organisations and individuals has become critical in the complexity of the structural changes being experienced in the reform of the public sector. The need for the achievement of set goals, calls for proper management systems to be put in place in order to facilitate the measurements of the results as well as to review that policy if it is dysfunctional. "Performance management approaches ensure that strategic directions are set for the achievement of desired results. Better planning, measuring and reporting is promoted".[19]

Policy development therefore includes all issues and aspects of the machinery and its human resources in the endeavour to respond to the needs of a changing society. Policy development and its management, in practice, is influenced by many factors which include the social and political environment; the state apparatus; the capacity of their institutions to implement policy once it is formulated; the relationship between elected and appointed officials (political and civil servants); performance measures; and key actors in the policy development process.

SOCIAL ENVIRONMENT

The social environment within which policy develops, includes the legal, ideological and type of administration. Any administration has its own unique organisation culture which is adopted over many years in implementing policies. The norms and values which guide the behaviour patterns of the human resources in work-places contribute to the way the policy is interpreted and meaningfully applied by the technocrats. The social environment, on which civil society organisations have a direct impact on policy development, is also influenced in its perception and analysis of the nature of the problem and the type of action appropriate for solution.

Experience has shown that laws can be passed by parliament only to be rejected by the civil society. It is also possible for Cabinet to formulate policies which may never be implemented and which may also be inconsistent with the value premises of society. Such policies are less likely to be implemented because of their non-conformity to the prevailing values and traditions of the community which is supposed to be the beneficiary of the services. The environment also takes into account the different political and economic philosophies expounded by the leading or ruling party which, in turn, is also influenced by international organisations within the context of global political economy.

The way the government is structured in readiness for policy development affects the pace and quality of policy formulation. While government may have genuine intentions about solving a particular problem through policy intervention strategies, the state machinery may be slow to implement perhaps because of its own cumbersome procedures, precedents, rules and regulations. Governments often complain about the slow pace at which development is taking place after policies have been formulated. In Zimbabwe, for example, President Robert Mugabe criticised some of his ministers, describing them as weak and slow to implement decisions and supervise their staff effectively. He said, "Finance Ministry is being accused of running a kind of a funeral parlour. I do not know what makes the Ministry resist implementation of decisions".[20] The criticism about his own government ministry was made in Botswana, a neighbouring country, in a brainstorming meeting between government leaders and private sector representatives attending the first Southern African Intenational Dialogue 1997 on Smart Partnership in Kasane. The statement clearly shows that there are certain policies which are being resisted and therefore not being implemented by the civil service.

ORGANISATIONAL STRUCTURE/STATE APPARATUS

Organisational structures in the public service tend to follow the customary or traditional vertical, pyramidal and hierarchical models with numerous grade levels based on seniority and length of service. Such models are functionally inappropriate to the requirements arising from decentralisation process, from the interest in starting up networks and promoting participation, and from the need to develop appropriate management styles. The style of management must suit the administrative changes, which include both vertical and lateral co-operation and collaboration with other agencies, in an attempt to make the new policy analysis framework function.

Among the problems created by the traditional bureaucratic structure, are that staff at senior levels tend to close in on themselves, turn routines into targets, develop serious resistance to the participation of other agents external to the structure, such as other possible partners and the recipient communities themselves, and can be extremely rigid in reacting to change.

The organisational structures should be re-organised to take into account the change imperatives on the organisation. Progress should be made towards more open, flexible and participatory structures. The design of organisational structures is not an end in itself, but a means to facilitating the achievement of objectives.

The re-organised structure should be underpinned by a management culture which respects the views of those junior to them, tolerates opposing views, is honest and reliable, has integrity and is free of corrupt and dictatorial tendencies. Top officials should not live in an ivory tower but should make themselves available and accessible to those who have direct contact with the client communities. The style and culture of management should aim to move towards the social reality and to react to change in the process of introducing new systems and instruments in the organisation.

In Britain, Plowden has acknowledged that there would always be tension between permanent officials and transient ministers in the implementation of policy decisions. He also noted that some governments were very suspicious of civil servants and consequently did not trust them.

Such complaints have, in some cases resulted in conflict between elected and appointed officials; between public and private sectors; between ministries and public enterprises; and between government and non-government organisations. The organisations and the administration of the state machinery are also critical in policy development, an issue which is often ignored in the whole policy management process (formulation, implementation, monitoring and evaluation).

While the infrastructure may have its own unique problems in policy development, the capacity of ministries, departments, public enterprises and individuals, may be questionable. An institution, for example, may not have the capacity to execute a policy programme because it does not have the capacity as exhibited by the lack of funding, resources, skills, knowledge and appropriate attitudes which are necessary to implement the policy.

INSTITUTIONAL CAPACITY

Institutional capacity has been identified by a number of international organisations, as being a critical factor to the whole process of policy development and management. This is particularly pertinent to situations in which nationals, with appropriate skills have left the country or have left the civil service. The flight of skills from the public sector depletes its resources and capacity to address the policy changes.

One of the key development challenges facing post-colonial Africa is the evolution of development policies and strategies which can adapt to a changing regional and global economy based on market liberalisation, technological change and rapid geo-political reconfiguration. Studies of the causes of Africa's slow growth and its economic marginalisation conclude that developing suitable human resource capacities to manage development, particularly policy formulation, is the critical requirement of future economic development and democratisation.[21]

The infrastructural and institutional incapacity in policy development and management has led some governments to rely very heavily on expatriates who may not be familiar with peculiarities of the development process of a particular country. A further problem associated with expatriates is that their contribution is purely technical and is not vested with the current thinking within the political and economic environment, resulting in a contradiction with the dominant values of civil society.

POLITICAL AND ADMINISTRATIVE BOUNDARIES

The poor division of functions and responsibilities between politicians and civil servants has contributed to confusion and silent conflict in the development of public policy. In many cases, political and administrative boundaries are not made explicitly clear to allow the incumbents of positions to know where their role begins and ends. The conflict between officials is often caused by a lack of clear boundaries leading to competition on the same resources and often resulting in accusations and counter-accusations between politicians and civil servants when policies are not being implemented. A clearly defined policy is necessary to assist the appropriate distribution of power and responsibilities in the management of resources.

In the United Kingdom, the newly elected Prime Minister, Tony Blair, defined the role of a politician. He said, "The people are the masters. We are the servants of the people. We will never forget that and, if we ever do, the people will very soon show that what the electorate gives the electorate can take away".[22]

PERFORMANCE MEASURES

The demands and expectations of civil society on the need to improve policy development and delivery have brought pressure to bear on the state to seek and maintain issues of equity, quality, quantity and coverage of the policy management. The characteristics sought of an effective and comprehensive service are defined as four measures of performance:

- Quantity – provides a comprehensive service.
- Quality – has a clarity of purpose, inherent logic, accuracy, range of options, adequate consultation and practicality of implementations.
- Time – meeting the reporting deadlines for projects.
- Cost – performed within agreed budgets.[23]

These performance policy measures are generally demanded by the consumers who are no longer passive but active in the policy development and management. Governments are therefore, expected to develop a policy which is relevant to its priorities of high quality and efficiently produced. In essence, the consumers expect value for money.

It should be realised that a meaningful and appropriate policy development depends on effective policy research and analysis, policy dialogue and above all training and the sharing of information amongst institutional policy centres, associations and individuals. The development of such a policy should ensure that the wider public is involved so as to develop an informed policy negotiation and choices.

KEY ACTORS IN STRATEGIC POLICY DEVELOPMENT

The social, political and economic environment within which policy development takes place is critical to the type and nature of the policy formulated. The environment is both the source and the recipient of the policy that is developed. Within the social environment are various competing, conflicting and collaborative institutions, individuals, and both formal and informal structures with an interest and a role in policy formation.

Within the formal structures are ministries, departments, public enterprises, parliament and Cabinet with its various committees responsible for many areas of government activity. While inter-ministerial committees are recognised, formal structures through which government policies are conceptualised, prepared and presented to Cabinet, they are by no means the best method of information-gathering in preparation for formal decision-making. The reason is that they do not, by the nature of their composition, have relevant expertise and skills in a particular discipline. Although they are representatives of interested ministries and departments, their composition in terms of level of authority fluctuates. In any one inter-ministerial committee, for example, the members attending may not be regular and, as a result, unfamiliar with the details of the previous discussions where briefing may not have been possible. The variation in attendance, therefore, does not contribute to consistency and continuity of policy ideas. However, the committees are necessary for consensus-building and the well-sought-after co-operation of ministries in the implementation process.

In order to enrich cabinet policy decisions, some countries, such as Zambia, Tanzania etc. have created Policy Analysis Review Units, whose purposes are to create and maintain data and to clarify the roles and responsibilities of policy functionaries within Ministries or within the co-ordinating agencies of government.

Civil society, in current thinking, is expected to contribute to policy development because of the economic and political liberalised policies adopted by many governments. Many functionaries would ask what is this civil society all about which is associated with the liberalisation of the economy and multi-party democracy. In general, "Civil society refers to organisations which are outside government but which find expression in their relationship to the state. Civil society denotes patterns of association, for example, single interest groups, professional associations and membership organisations. Organs of civil society are therefore heterogeneous. Their purposes, constitution and envisaged duration vary. All are, in one way or another, interest groups that may, for example, represent a particular sectoral interest (farmers, chambers of commerce, trade unions) or a particular policy point view (pressure groups). Together they constitute the mechanism by which a diverse range of views are directed at public policy-makers and absorbed into the consultative process. They provide an opportunity to influence the direction of government policy without necessarily seeking political office. They constitute a link between the individual and the state."[24]

Civil society as part of the informal structure, therefore, contributes to policy formation. Many governments have found it essential to involve civil society as a way of developing a national consensus in anticipation of acceptance or approval of policy outcome. Accountability by the government and acceptance of policy by civil society is a guarantee that the policy is solid, comprehensive and all-embracing.

The external pressures and actors, consisting of international and regional organisations, non-government organisations and significant others contribute to policy formation through their own influences; the provision of information and data; the supply of technical assistance; and the spread of philosophies and success stories. Amongst the most influential, external sources of government policies are the donors, through their expertise, technology and aid. This is especially the case in circumstances where there is poor policy infrastructural and institutional capacity, an absence of local and national expertise and a lack of a well-organised civil society.

POLICY DEVELOPMENT PROCESS

The process of formulating a policy varies from one country to the other and does not necessarily follow the same path to final decision-taking. However, in general, there are essential steps that are recognised and usually followed by policy analysts and public managers in varying propositions, depending on unique circumstances.

The first step is to identify an issue or a problem that has to be addressed or solved. The way in which the problem has been conceptualised, the identified group experiencing the problem, the people who have identified the problem, their interests and the social environment within which the issue has been identified, are all critical factors that facilitate the identification and conceptualisation of the problem. The nature of the policy formulated depends on a number of factors, including the pressures for change; stakes involved in change; level of decision-makers involved; existence of precedents; interests of external forces; the degree of change; the threats to the status quo; the method of identification and the time within which it is conceptualised. The process therefore addresses questions of who, when, what, why and how.

The institutional environment from which the policy issues may arise does affect the way the issue is conceptualised and articulated. Their response, for example, to the Economic Structural Adjustment Programme has depended on the type of environment in which it is introduced. In some countries, there has been resistance, while in others it has been regarded as an inevitable change with the support of influential groups in society.

The second step is related to the setting up of clearly defined goals and objectives for addressing an issue or for solving a particular identified problem. The process of stating the goals equally involves a lot of other stakeholders who may either lose or benefit from such a change. The defined objectives are influenced by the political economic and social environment in which they are prioritised and for which funding for solutions of the problem is made available.

Experience has shown that for policy formulation to be meaningful the goals have to be clearly identified so that action-oriented strategies for solution become appropriate. This will avoid the danger of formulating a policy which does not address the real problem and issues. In making goals explicit, it is possible to determine the resources needed, the time-frame, the technology and the skills required, the methodology of investigation and the data required.

The third step is the formulation of alternative courses of action and making choices out of the options. The making of choices is one of the difficult steps in the whole process of policy development. Due care and thorough consideration is necessary as experience has shown that the solution of one problem can create another unanticipated problem. The choices can also be made complicated by the existence of many actors in the policy formulation process since different people perceive issues differently and place different interpretations on policy outcome. In making choices, the policy analysts would argue that the advantages and disadvantages of each option should be spelt out to assist policy-makers. Policy decisions are therefore made after the ideological and methodological issues have been examined and the statistical data provided.

The fourth step is the designing of the implementation stage once the policy decision has been made. Some legal and administrative instruments would have to be put in place so that the information can be disseminated to the public and the target groups. In designing the strategies, consideration has to be given to the instruments that implement the change, the financial and human resources that facilitated the process would have to be made explicit so that roles can be clearly delineated. Often, polices are formulated but funding is not made available or there are no skilled people to perform the required functions.

The last stage relates to the monitoring of the policy while it is being implemented for purposes of finding out what needs to be done to ensure that the policy remains on track and is meeting the target clientele. The monitoring process is followed by a review of the policy after a certain period in the implementation process.

BEST PRACTICE GUIDELINES FOR POLICY ANALYSIS AND MANAGEMENT FRAMEWORK

Brief but comprehensive and easy-to-follow and understand guidelines will assist in firmly installing the policy analysis and management framework into the entire organisational structure of government. The guidelines are designed to improve the quality of policy analysis, lessen misunderstandings about the framework, promote a joint-ownership approach between the centre of government and its agencies, and those who will use the policy framework once it is in place.

An example of the contents of policy analysis and management guidelines are given below:

1. Ensure links with decision-making processes

Policy analysis can be an important stage in policy formulation as it improves the quality of policy intervention and the budget process to support priorities and savings. Appropriate policy measurement instruments address issues that are significant for political, budgetary, management and other strategic reasons.

Objectives of policy analysis determine location, methodology and use of evaluation. Policy analysis should be tailored to the characteristics of a policy intervention and the methodology should suit the objectives of the intended policy.

Planning improves policy analysis since it includes objectives, criteria, data collection and methods.

2. Foster policy analysis and management culture

Support for policy analysis is demonstrated through the willingness of politicians, policy managers and central government agencies.

Demand for policy analysis needs to be generated, specified and articulated by internal and external stakeholders. Policy analysis without ownership by stakeholders is unlikely to have an effect. Institutional barriers to policy analysis, such as internal resistance, can be reduced through consultation, aiming at creating mutual trust.

The government can support a policy analysis culture that encourages innovation and adaptation to a changing environment. The basic message should be that to stay relevant, organisations need to continue learning from analysis and feedback about the results.

Training and professional dialogue, competent analysts, well-informed permanent secretaries and ministers, and enlightened and enthusiastic users all contribute to policy analysis culture.

3. Enhance credibility

Factors influencing credibility include the competence and credibility of the policy analysts; mutual trust between the analysts and those whose work is analysed; consultation and involvement of stakeholders; and processes for communicating the findings and conclusions.

Professional and ethical standards, and methodological quality of policy analysis (encompassing issues such as relevant criteria, adequate evidence and reliable and clear findings) also have an effect on the credibility of policy analysis. Quality assurance and open and frank dialogue can improve credibility by exposing and rectifying potential weakness in policy development and management.

4. Managing policy analysis activities strategically

Organisation of policy analysis should correspond to needs and priorities in different policy areas. It may be appropriate to systematise and institutionalise policy analysis in key policy areas where the costs of collecting data is high and information limited.

Central government agencies play an important role in managing the policy analysis and development process; however, the actual policy analysis and development can be decentralised to different actors at all levels of government.

Development of policy analysis and management skills in different organisation ensures the necessary range of analytical methods and perspectives (e.g. drawing from both internal and external analysts), and that each policy analysis is designed in accordance with its unique set of issues related to objectives, focus, credibility and intended use.

Special funds for financing policy analysis and development can serve as an important incentive for analysing public policies; however, they may also serve to encourage use of policy analysis when other performance management approaches may be more appropriate.[25]

INSTITUTIONALISATION OF THE POLICY ANALYSIS FRAMEWORK

When all the policy development processes have been completed, policy instruments and systems designed, best practice guidelines formulated, and the organisation restructured to accommodate the change process, there is a need to ensure that the new system is incorporated into the total organisation so that it becomes sustainable. It should be mentioned that the incorporation of the new system, while desirable, may meet with resistance from within the organisation, especially those agents who may be threatened by the new policy framework. In this regard, due care should be taken to ensure that the new system is appropriately institutionalised. For the institutionalisation or internalisation process to be successful, the following should be taken into account:

Location: The new policy framework should be located in the Head of Government offices, such as the President, or Prime Minister and Cabinet, to become an important part of the centre of government.

Authority and power: In order for the framework to be respected, especially by heads of ministries who report to the centre in their own individual way, it should be given the authority to co-ordinate with ministries directly. This can be done by Cabinet Office issuing a directive that all policies must pass through the policy analysis unit.

CO-ORDINATION ROLE

While the policy unit has power and authority to execute its duties, it should also be regarded as a co-ordinating instrument, in matters of policy, to assist the Head of State to take an appropriate decision. The co-ordinating role should include consultation; communication; collaboration; and co-operation with those ministries it is supposed to work with. The co-ordinating role contributes to the reduction of duplication, confusion, competition and conflicts between and among ministries, departments and other agencies.

RANK AND CAREER STRUCTURE

Once the policy unit has been established, it should be staffed by professionally competent personnel with a career structure compatible with the civil service structure. It should be seen as part of the system and not divorced from it, as this can create hostility between and among other agents of government. The rank of head of the policy unit should be that of permanent secretary or head of ministry for ease of co-operation at a colleague level with heads of ministries. The staff, in the unit, should have a potential for lateral or vertical transfer to other departments of government and should not feel that this is a dead end job.

POLICY CO-ORDINATING UNITS IN SECTORAL MINISTRIES

For the policy unit to be effective, it is suggested that small policy units be established in other ministries for ease of co-ordination. The units in ministries, while being accountable to their heads of ministries, should have a direct link with the Policy Analysis Unit in Cabinet Office. The ministerial policy unit would be responsible for co-ordinating all of a ministry's policies, including the departments and public enterprises in that ministry.

TRAINING AND DEVELOPMENT

By far the most important instrument for accelerating the institutionalisation process is the continuous training of the staff and management development for the top officials. The staff in the policy unit, should always upgrade their skills and knowledge in research, planning, monitoring and evaluation. They should also be in a position to use the latest instruments in technology, such as computers and other communication technologies.

Training contributes to behavioural and attitudinal change as well as breaking down of barriers, resistance and rigidities. The training programme should focus not only on their daily activities but also on change management policy decision-making processes; inter-governmental co-ordination; and civil society's organisations such as labour, unions, interest groups, professional staff associations such as teachers, nurses and lawyers and other non-government or community-based organisations.

USE OF EXTERNAL SIGNIFICANT ORGANISATIONS AND INSTITUTIONS

The policy analysis unit should be able to tap the knowledge, skills and information from national universities, colleges, management institutes and other institutions of higher learning. They can also work closely with regional organisations that deal with research, policy and planning issues. The Southern African Regional Institute for Policy Studies based in Harare, is one such institution that policy units could make use of in the region.

Figure 1

Pressures for Rethinking Policy Analysis

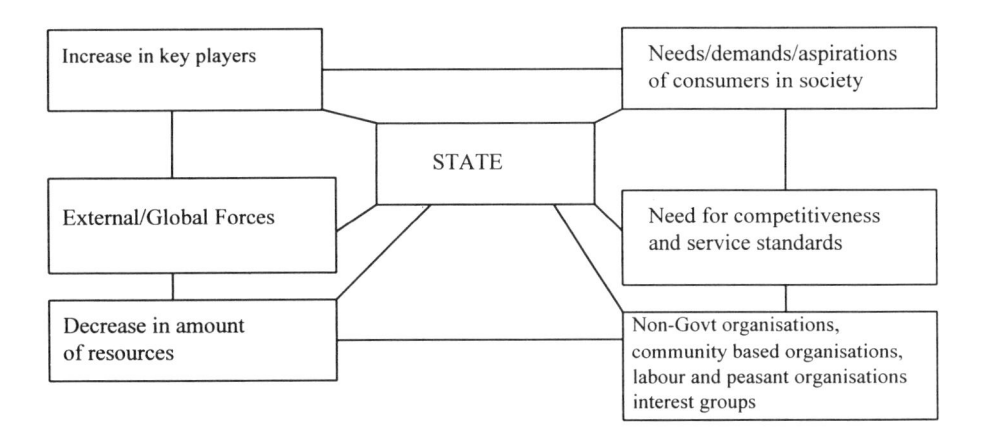

```
┌─────────────────────────┐                      ┌─────────────────────────┐
│ Increase in key players │──────────────────────│ Needs/demands/aspirations│
│                         │                      │ of consumers in society │
└─────────────────────────┘                      └─────────────────────────┘
             │                                                │
             │              ┌─────────────┐                   │
             │              │    STATE    │                   │
┌─────────────────────────┐ └─────────────┘  ┌─────────────────────────┐
│ External/Global Forces  │                  │ Need for competitiveness│
│                         │                  │ and service standards   │
└─────────────────────────┘                  └─────────────────────────┘
             │                                                │
┌─────────────────────────┐                  ┌─────────────────────────────┐
│ Decrease in amount      │──────────────────│ Non-Govt organisations,     │
│ of resources            │                  │ community based organisations,│
└─────────────────────────┘                  │ labour and peasant organisations│
                                             │ interest groups             │
                                             └─────────────────────────────┘
```

Result

- Change in Policy Management Paradigm
- new policy analysis framework
- things done differently
- meaningful utilisation of resources

Figure 2

Methodological Issues and Path to Policy Selection Mechanisms

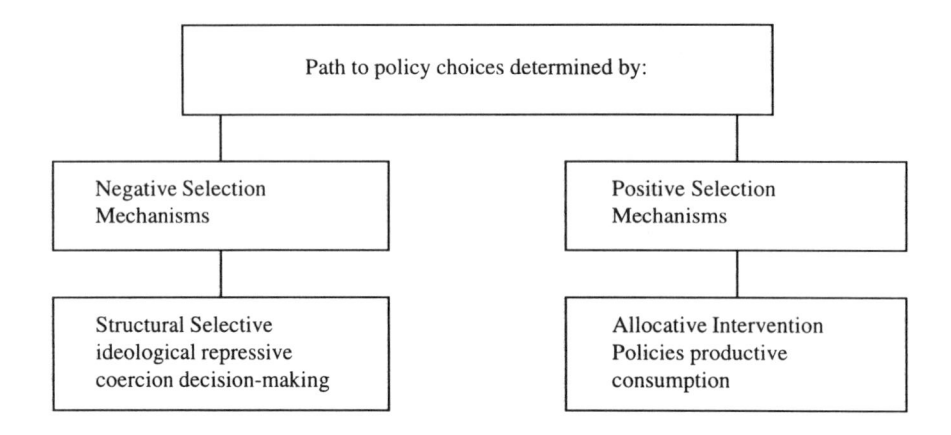

```
┌─────────────────────────────────────────────┐
│     Path to policy choices determined by:   │
└─────────────────────────────────────────────┘
         │                          │
┌──────────────────────┐   ┌──────────────────────┐
│ Negative Selection   │   │ Positive Selection   │
│ Mechanisms           │   │ Mechanisms           │
└──────────────────────┘   └──────────────────────┘
         │                          │
┌──────────────────────┐   ┌──────────────────────┐
│ Structural Selective │   │ Allocative Intervention│
│ ideological repressive│  │ Policies productive  │
│ coercion decision-making│ │ consumption         │
└──────────────────────┘   └──────────────────────┘
```

Results:

- framework determined by the nature of the problem
- framework dictated by the availability of resources
- social inclusion of different actors in the process
- linked to nature and type of organisational structure
- policy strategies have an ideological base
- social environment undergoing change

Figure 3

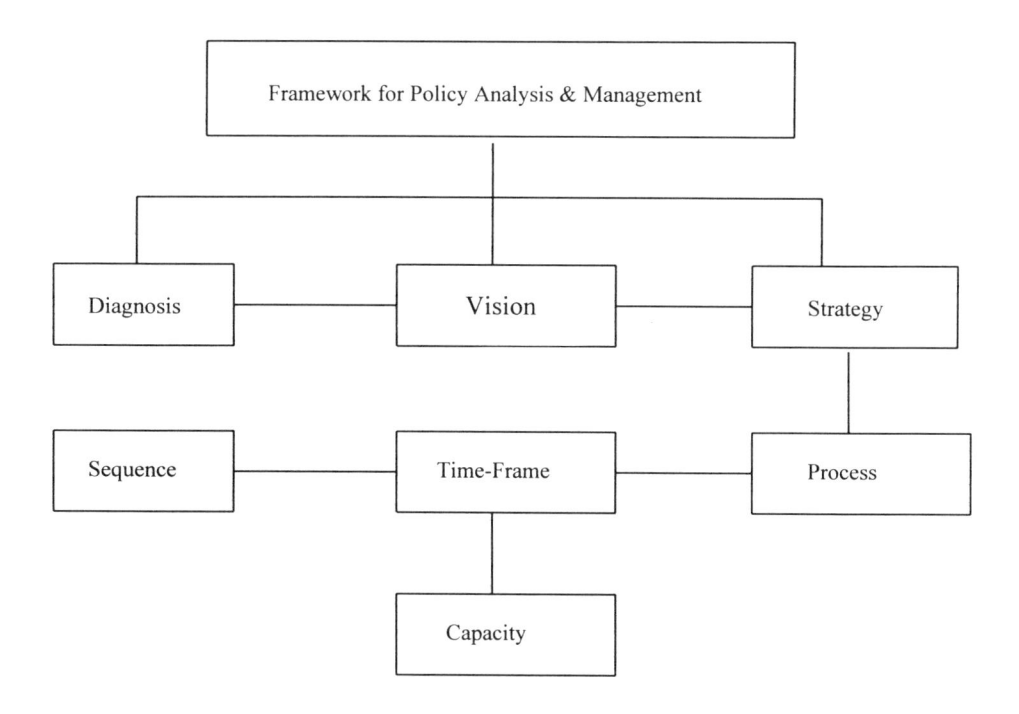

```
                ┌─────────────────────────────────────────────┐
                │    Framework for Policy Analysis & Management │
                └─────────────────────────────────────────────┘
                                     │
        ┌────────────────────────────┼────────────────────────────┐
    ┌───────────┐              ┌───────────┐              ┌───────────┐
    │ Diagnosis │──────────────│   Vision  │──────────────│  Strategy │
    └───────────┘              └───────────┘              └───────────┘
                                                                │
    ┌───────────┐              ┌───────────┐              ┌───────────┐
    │  Sequence │──────────────│ Time-Frame│              │  Process  │
    └───────────┘              └───────────┘              └───────────┘
                                     │
                               ┌───────────┐
                               │  Capacity │
                               └───────────┘
```

Essential Questions to guide the Process:

1. Where are we?

2. Where do we want to go?

3. Why do we want to go there?

4. How do we get there?

5. With what resources?

6. When do we hope to get there?

Figure 4

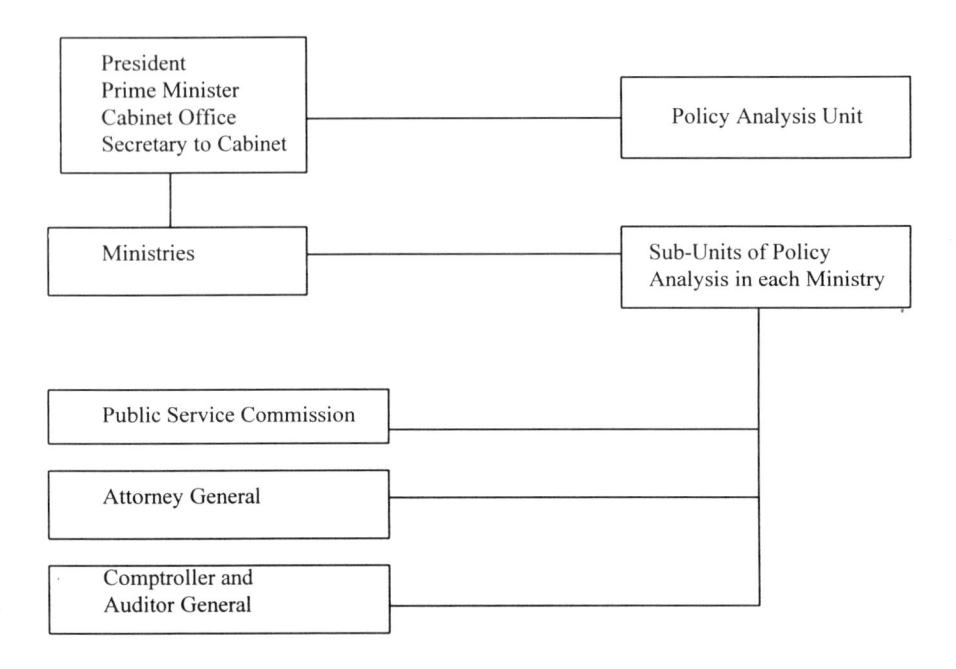

Institutionalisation of Policy Framework

```
┌─────────────────────┐
│ President           │
│ Prime Minister      │──────────────┐   ┌──────────────────────┐
│ Cabinet Office      │              ├───│ Policy Analysis Unit │
│ Secretary to Cabinet│              │   └──────────────────────┘
└──────────┬──────────┘              │
           │                         │
┌──────────┴──────────┐              │   ┌──────────────────────┐
│ Ministries          │──────────────┼───│ Sub-Units of Policy  │
└─────────────────────┘              │   │ Analysis in each     │
                                     │   │ Ministry             │
                                     │   └──────────┬───────────┘
┌─────────────────────────┐          │              │
│ Public Service Commission│─────────┼──────────────┤
└─────────────────────────┘          │              │
┌─────────────────────┐              │              │
│ Attorney General    │──────────────┼──────────────┤
└─────────────────────┘              │              │
┌─────────────────────┐              │              │
│ Comptroller and     │──────────────┴──────────────┘
│ Auditor General     │
└─────────────────────┘
```

Criteria

Visible benefits and costs
Foster policy management culture
Credibility of staff in the policy unit
Trust between and among senior staff
Good communication skills
Efforts for collaboration and co-operation
Consultation process
Appropriate remunerations of staff
Career structure
Possible lateral and vertical advancement

MODELS OF POLICY ANALYSIS AND MANAGEMENT

As stated in the text, policy analysis and development management frameworks by themselves alone are no panacea to the solutions of management problems. They are only a facilitator or catalyst to the successful development and management of policy. They are simply a structured way of thinking about choices before deciding on a particular choice of action. They constitute an instrument or mechanism by which policy can be analysed, developed and managed. Since they are a product, or ought to be a product of each country, they vary in different proportions to the interest, culture and experiences of the individuals and organisations.

The following models are provided here as examples only.

BOTSWANA

The Botswana Public Service has 72,000 posts (excluding the army) in a population of 1.3 million. It is based firmly on the British system from which it continues to draw in the context of public service reform in general and such new innovations as "Work Improvement Teams" and "Productivity Improvement Committees". The Botswana Public Service has always sustained a level of improvement and efficiency in its delivery system, thanks to both the availability of growing economic and financial resources in this very rich country, and a determined commitment to training and development. The relative smallness of the government itself, the closeness and near homogeneity of the Botswana community itself, and a leadership that has thrived on a commendable regard for the values and norms of a good public service – all these have made the Botswana Public Service in particular, and the Government of the Republic of Botswana in general, the best possible model in the context of the problems that are attendant to the post-colonial state in Africa.

With respect to Botswana's experience in co-ordination and collaboration at the level of government, this centres on the relationship between the Ministries of Finance and Public Service, the structure of the Cabinet and its Committees, the role of the President himself, and the Committees that facilitate close liaison in policy matters within and between key sectors of the government system.[26] The Botswana Cabinet meets weekly, a contributory factor to co-ordination and collaboration. However, this is enhanced by the system of preparatory work that is considered a necessary precondition for cabinet discussions on new policies. If any ministry wants to come up with a policy, it is circulated in the form of a memorandum which is submitted to a Business Committee comprising the Permanent Secretary to the President and Cabinet, the Attorney General and the Permanent Secretary for Finance. If the policy issue has obvious financial and personnel implications, the Ministries of Finance and Public Service will have to have consultations and make the necessary recommendations to the Business Committee. These two ministries have a good working relationship and have been able to institute "manpower sub-committees" in all ministries, enhancing the level of collaboration between the two ministries on such issues as the downsizing or right-sizing of the public service. Likewise, such committees as the "Work Improvement Team" are devoted to the development of human resources and to encouraging respective departments towards resolving their own problems. There is also a "Productivity Improvement Committee" for the civil service as a whole.

The Ministries of Finance and Public Service, therefore, constitute the two key strategic resource departments for the public service. They work together in policy-making, since policy has to be integrated into the budget development process. The budget itself has to be aligned with the strategic focus of government. The two ministries have to collaborate in measuring performance, progress and impact. They must indicate objectives, strategies and resources. Donor funding will have to be in accordance with strategic planning and goals; and unlike in other Southern African countries in which donors appear to be calling the shots and causing distortions in policy direction, Botswana has been able to decline such aid as it considers inimical to the strategies and goals of its public service and government. There are determined attempts at reducing reliance on donors. Equally important, the two departments also have outward linkages; they link with the provinces and districts without necessarily seeking to control them.

Botswana's "philosophy of development" is contained and reflected in the National Development Plan, as the indicator of the direction which the government has chosen, and as an outcome of the broadest consultation possible within the society. The budget itself is guided by the Development Plan, and the latter underpins the budget with the "philosophy". This is an outstanding achievement for Botswana in a sub-region – and in a continent – in which Development Plans have all but disappeared in recent years. By the 1980s, they had become meaningless. This was in large measure due to the growing dominance of donors who are now demanding matching funds, often at the expense of the entire capital budget of a given country. The social deficit becomes too large and therefore difficult to prioritise. In effect, the donor has become the planner. As has already been explained, the extent to which most African countries now have no Development Plans is a reflection of a post-colonial state under siege, with fewer and fewer options, increasingly dependent on the *external*, and struggling to survive.

Some concluding remarks on the "Botswana model which will need further elaboration in the form of a workshop on the subject. The first refers to the role of the Business Committee consisting of the Permanent Secretary to the President and Cabinet, the Attorney General and the Permanent Secretary for Finance. As has already been mentioned, this Committee serves as an important "clearing house" for policy initiatives, ensures co-ordination and collaboration in the exercise of policy formulation and evaluation, and constitutes a vital link between the civil servants as an integral component in policy-making, and the President and Cabinet as the executive authority of government. The model is not only a screening system; it is a more "scientific" system of getting things to Cabinet. The circulation of memoranda ensures that all ministries contribute some ideas irrespective of the subject.

There is, therefore, a lively relationship between the key sectors of government.

The second refers to the role of the President himself and how this enhances the content of co-ordination and collaboration, breaking down artificial barriers that often accompany bureaucratic structures and procedures, and keeping the Head of State in touch with reality. In Botswana, the Permanent Secretaries meet with the President once a month. Unlike in other countries in the region where the executive loses touch with problems on the ground, the meeting between the President and his Permanent Secretaries also gives the latter a sense of confidence while keeping them on their toes.

Thirdly, there is also a level of decentralisation of functions: recruitment is done at ministry level and then approved by a "Manpower Sub-Committee". A rural development council, chaired by the Vice President, co-ordinates rural affairs and incorporates local government, traditional leaders and structure. There is a central Joint Staff Consultative Council to oversee employer/employee relations, including policy initiatives. Ministers tour the whole country in order to explain policy initiatives and the budget allocation system to the people.

Lastly, there is also in Botswana a Directorate on Corruption and Economic crime being set up. This Directorate has a centre at headquarters where anyone may report. This is an important institution which, if effectively put in place, can contain the growing threat of corruption in most African countries, enhance confidence in the conduct and integrity of public officials, and improve the moral fabric of society.

ZAMBIA

The Zambian model was conceptualised and designed after experiencing many problems relating to the management of policy. The following were the major problems and concerns experienced by both public servants and politicians as shown by the case study on Policy Change.[27]

1. After the fall of copper prices, the government continued to spend more than it generated, resulting in rising budget deficits and growing overseas debt. By the early 1990s, the country's economy was on the verge of collapse. Government stores, for example, were sparsely stocked and basic government services such as education and health care had all but disintegrated.

2. In addition to the lack of public accountability during Kaunda's term of office, were poor formal systems for making and implementing policy.

Rather than benefiting from the perspective and analysis of technical experts, policy formulation and decision-making were centralised in the office of the President and ruling party headquarters (UNIP) where decisions were based more on socialist dogma than a careful analysis of problems or objectives and possible actions to address them.

3. The civil servants in ministries had become increasingly marginalised from the policy processes. They began to avoid risk and conflict with politicians and consequently deferred even the most routine decisions upwards. As they were not involved in the decision-making processes, they developed little ownership, understanding and commitment to the implementation or follow-up of government policy decisions.

4. The morale of civil servants was very low as they could be fired and transferred at short notice and sometimes without alternatives to appeal against such arbitrary decisions. At the national elections, Kaunda's party lost and in came the new government of Chiluba. The new government inherited the old civil servants and their machineries. The new government, eager to make meaningful contribution to the development of national policies, soon experienced problems in formulating and implementing government policy decisions. The following managerial problems were experienced.

- A major constraint was that new ministers lacked experience. Because ministers' roles and functions were not clearly defined or agreed upon, confusion over the authority of Cabinet ministers to formulate policy or publicly comment on government policies created the image of a government in disarray. It was not uncommon for ministers to make conflicting policy statements publicly.

- Because Cabinet itself did not require well-thought-out policy proposals, there was no impetus for those in line ministries to devote time or effort to developing them. Few ministries possessed career civil servants well versed in even the rudiments of policy analysis.

- Further hindering sound policy formulation was the fact that few ministries maintained data bases for their functional areas of responsibility. This meant that no tradition of monitoring the performance of programmes and policies existed.

- The lack of clarity about roles, responsibilities and authority created tension within the ministries. Particularly difficult to sort out were the lines of authority and relationship between ministers and their permanent secretaries. Thus, rather than constituting balanced teams comprising a mix of players versed in both the technical and political aspects of policy development and implementation, the climate in ministries often resembled turf wars or silent struggles dedicated to testing who had the authority to tell whom what to do.[28]

In some cases policy proposals were drafted by foreign technical experts on behalf of the sponsoring ministry, but these often lacked the necessary political, contextual or technical perspective to make implementation possible. The process of developing and managing a policy is reflected in Figure one. The framework, as can be seen, had serious flaws in its design and capacity to analyse and manage efficiently a policy that is formulated. Because of the inherent constraints exhibited by the system, ministries were able to implement about 25% of Cabinet decisions. The remaining decisions were either not implemented or were only partially implemented.

Clearly, the system could not sustain any structural changes or reforms of the state machinery in order to address the growing demand from citizens for better quality of service, productivity and promotion of good governance, the ticket under which the present government was elected into power. The support of an emerging democratic process and institutions was lacking and exacerbated by the inability to co-ordinate the formulation of policy and the absence of well-trained public servants in policy management. On realising and identifying the problems in policy formulation and management and the limitations of administrative structures to sustain the implementation of policy, the government hired a team of consultants whose objectives were:

- to develop a system of analysing policy proposals submitted to Cabinet by ministries and to assess their consistency with government policy;

- to suggest ways of improving the co-ordination and implementation of policy;

- to monitor the decisions of Cabinet.

These objectives were discussed at a number of workshops held in the country. Different workshops were held for top officials in government, permanent secretaries and cabinet ministers. All the workshops concluded that there was a need to improve the framework for policy formulation, decision-making, policy implementation and policy monitoring or evaluation.

Out of these workshops and discussions, the Policy Analysis and Co-ordination Division was established in the Cabinet office. The division was established following the merger of the then two existing divisions in Cabinet office namely, the Economics and Finance and Cabinet Affairs. Further workshops were held in order to implement the new framework which would improve the effectiveness of government by providing the Cabinet with high quality advice and assisting the Cabinet to co-ordinate and implement policies. Two conclusions were drawn from the workshops. The first was that the Policy Analysis and Co-ordination (PAC) Division would act as a facilitator or broker in the policy process without controlling powers. Obviously, the role would require skills not only in policy analysis but also in facilitation and systems development.

The second conclusion reached was that improving policy-making and implementation within the Zambian context required commitment at the top. Specifically, far-reaching changes would not come about simply because PAC will them to be so. High-level support was also needed. Only Cabinet possessed the power to push the policy process a level higher by demanding higher quality policy proposals and implementation from ministries.

The new policy process as shown in figure 2 is clearly a framework or model designed by the Zambians themselves through the interactions of various stakeholders. The framework reflects the ownership by the Zambians who understand how it should operate.

The following are a few lessons which have been learnt from establishing the PAC and from its implementation during its first few years in existence. These include:

1. **A complete national policy process is needed (capabilities and systems for formulating, deciding on, implementing, and monitoring/ evaluating the impact of policy).** Policy formulation/analysis requires reliable data and the ability to interpret that data (monitoring and evaluation skills and systems). Sound policy decision-making depends on good analysis and a straightforward presentation to decision-makers of the policy alternatives and their probable outcomes. And the foundation upon which the implementation of policy is built is well-founded, clearly-articulated decisions and their communication to those responsible for implementation. Because each stage of the policy process depends on the others, it is necessary to devote time to identifying and then addressing weaknesses in the process, whether they occur in the formulation, decision-making, implementation or monitoring/evaluation stages.

2. **As much attention needs to be given to policy implementation as is customarily given to "the decision".** The process of formulating policy and gaining support for policy proposals consumes so much effort that often there appears to be little energy left to deal with the implementation of the policy decision, let alone assess the impact of past policy decisions. Old habits die hard, but training in monitoring and evaluation has been a useful means of focusing attention on these important, post-decision activities. That phenomenon is hardly limited to developing country governments.

3. **Co-ordinating a policy process requires the existence of both systems and skills.** Systems are required to ensure that each policy conceived is the product of a thorough and inclusive analytical process. Routines must also be established for putting policy decisions into action and assessing their impact. Among the necessary skills needed in a co-ordinating agency such as PAC are analytic skills, such as policy analysis and monitoring/evaluation techniques. Less obvious, but equally necessary, are skills in dealing effectively with a variety of actors at a number of levels of rank or seniority; building commitment to change; and assessing inefficiencies or weaknesses in the national policy system.

4. **The implementation of new policies often requires organisations to behave differently.** If organisations are expected to behave differently, so too must the people who staff them – this is often the biggest challenge. Systems are relatively easy to change. Changing the attitudes and behaviour of those within the organisations is much more difficult to accomplish. "Attitudes and behaviour" in this context refers to methods of interacting with others of both higher and lower rank within the organisation; interacting with representatives of other organisations or groups; and making decisions setting organisational priorities, recognising excellence, settling disputes, etc.

5. **The implementation of even simple policies often requires the co-ordination and co-operation of multiple organisations.** Since many organisations are not accustomed to collaborating or co-ordinating their actions with other organisations, this behaviour needs to become part of organisations' normal operating routine and culture of the organisations.

6. **Strengthening a "co-ordinating agency," such as PAC, may be necessary to improve the performance of a national policy process, but it is not sufficient if the agencies that hold primary responsibility for policy formulation and implementation are weak.** There is an obvious difference in the potential contribution of an agency, like PAC, that co-ordinates the implementation of well-founded policy and one that doggedly works to implement poorly-conceived policies. It is on these grounds that considerable work has been done to improve ministries' capabilities to produce quality policy proposals, and at least a portion of training resources under this project have been programmed towards strengthening the policy analytical skills of select individuals in each ministry.

7. **It is important for co-ordinating agencies to understand their stakeholders.** Part of the challenge for PAC in designing improvements to Zambia's policy process has been creating systems that both demonstrate an appreciation of the interests of PAC's major stakeholders (the Cabinet ministers and the civil servants in the ministries) and gently

challenge these stakeholders to a higher level of performance. With Cabinet ministers, this meant creating a system through which Cabinet received better information upon which to base its decisions. In "exchange" for this, it is the expectation that ministers will abide by the new rules that they themselves endorsed (i.e. not seek special exceptions to excuse themselves and their policy proposals from proper co-ordination and policy analysis). For their part, the new system gives civil servants a greater and more meaningful role in the development and implementation of government policy; but at the same time, it places upon them the burden of conducting thorough analysis and co-ordination to support their policy recommendations. Rather than being responsible for merely submitting papers to Cabinet for consideration, they are expected to produce results.

8. **Senior civil servants need to be trained in organisational management.** For example, permanent secretaries of ministries often achieve their position by virtue of either their tenure in the civil service, their knowledge of "the system," and/or their sectoral knowledge. While some people can become good managers without the benefit of formal management training, it is perhaps unrealistic to expect across-the-board improvements in the civil service to take place without some attention being given to training in how to manage an effective organisation and how to lead a change process. Management and leadership skills are acquired and not necessarily innate.

9. **The sequencing and timing of project events is important.** It is sometimes tempting to go for the "big event" early in a project. For example, the first workshop held for permanent secretaries of ministries was held according to the terms of the contract – some six months into the contract and four months after PAC was established. Despite this, the consensus is that this workshop may have occurred prematurely. The difficulties encountered at the PS workshop were mostly due to PAC "going public" before gaining a firm grounding in what needed to be said and decided. In addition, very little time preceding the permanent secretary workshop was built into the project for the technical assistance staff to conduct detailed systems analysis and diagnostics. In contrast, the workshop for Cabinet ministers was held at an appropriate juncture in the project (over a year after the project commenced). Proper research had been conducted. Issues were identified that required attention and decision. Solid proposals were ready for presentation and discussion.

10. **The principles of strategic management are useful in both policy development and implementation.** Having said that, stating objectives, assessing stakeholder interests, evaluating organisational capacities, developing strategies etc. are not actions that public sector managers may automatically turn to – even if these concepts have been presented and

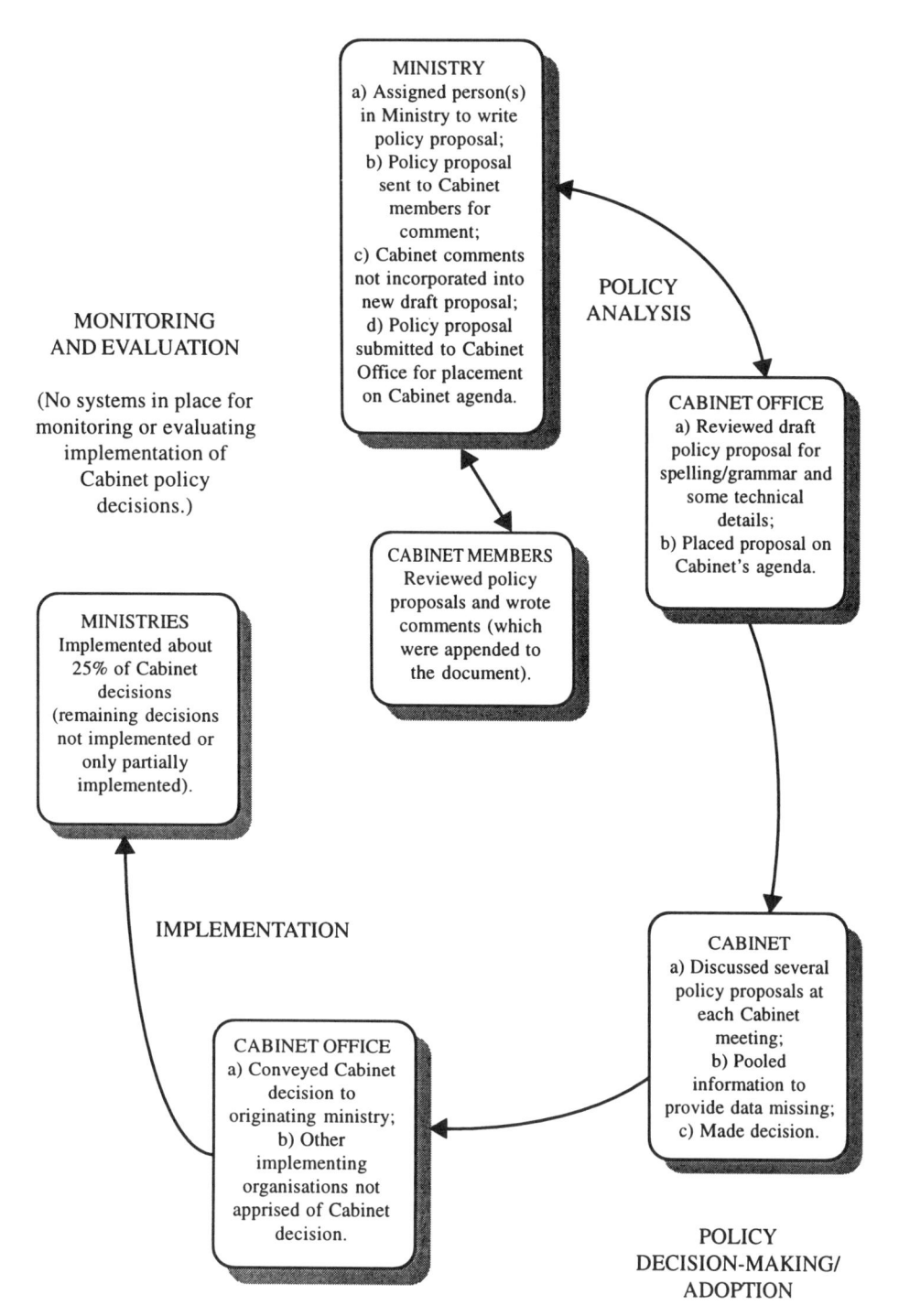

ZAMBIAN POLICY PROCESS BEFORE PROJECT   Figure 1

MINISTRY
a) Assigned person(s) in Ministry to write policy proposal;
b) Policy proposal sent to Cabinet members for comment;
c) Cabinet comments not incorporated into new draft proposal;
d) Policy proposal submitted to Cabinet Office for placement on Cabinet agenda.

POLICY ANALYSIS

MONITORING AND EVALUATION

(No systems in place for monitoring or evaluating implementation of Cabinet policy decisions.)

CABINET OFFICE
a) Reviewed draft policy proposal for spelling/grammar and some technical details;
b) Placed proposal on Cabinet's agenda.

CABINET MEMBERS
Reviewed policy proposals and wrote comments (which were appended to the document).

MINISTRIES
Implemented about 25% of Cabinet decisions (remaining decisions not implemented or only partially implemented).

IMPLEMENTATION

CABINET OFFICE
a) Conveyed Cabinet decision to originating ministry;
b) Other implementing organisations not apprised of Cabinet decision.

CABINET
a) Discussed several policy proposals at each Cabinet meeting;
b) Pooled information to provide data missing;
c) Made decision.

POLICY DECISION-MAKING/ ADOPTION

NEW GRZ POLICY PROCESS Figure 2

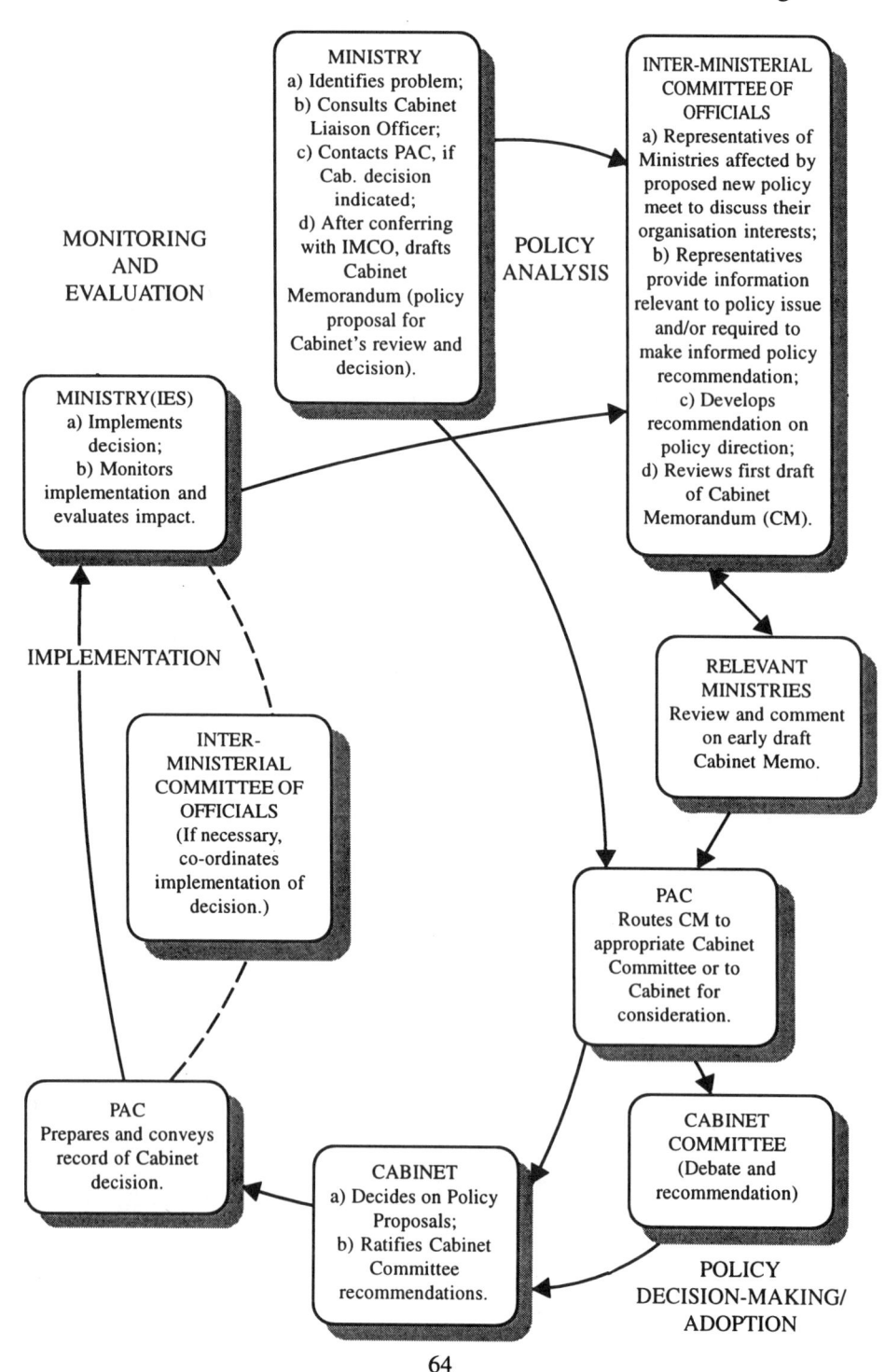

MINISTRY
a) Identifies problem;
b) Consults Cabinet Liaison Officer;
c) Contacts PAC, if Cab. decision indicated;
d) After conferring with IMCO, drafts Cabinet Memorandum (policy proposal for Cabinet's review and decision).

INTER-MINISTERIAL COMMITTEE OF OFFICIALS
a) Representatives of Ministries affected by proposed new policy meet to discuss their organisation interests;
b) Representatives provide information relevant to policy issue and/or required to make informed policy recommendation;
c) Develops recommendation on policy direction;
d) Reviews first draft of Cabinet Memorandum (CM).

MONITORING AND EVALUATION

POLICY ANALYSIS

MINISTRY(IES)
a) Implements decision;
b) Monitors implementation and evaluates impact.

RELEVANT MINISTRIES Review and comment on early draft Cabinet Memo.

IMPLEMENTATION

INTER-MINISTERIAL COMMITTEE OF OFFICIALS
(If necessary, co-ordinates implementation of decision.)

PAC Routes CM to appropriate Cabinet Committee or to Cabinet for consideration.

PAC Prepares and conveys record of Cabinet decision.

CABINET
a) Decides on Policy Proposals;
b) Ratifies Cabinet Committee recommendations.

CABINET COMMITTEE (Debate and recommendation)

POLICY DECISION-MAKING/ ADOPTION

discussed. At least in the PAC context, strategic management seems to be more of a practice skill. Creating the strategic management "state of mind" in public managers (making its application second nature or automatic) requires successive rounds of introduction to and practice in these principles.

It is clear from the discussion that the conceptualisation, formulation and design of the policy analysis instrument, the implementation and evaluation process were owned and led by the Zambians themselves. While they needed external catalysts in funding and development of the system, they controlled and directed the process. In essence, the process was dictated by the need to address a policy management problem and by the desire to promote good governance, public accountability, efficiency, effectiveness and above all to improve the delivery of better quality services to the majority of the population. The Zambian model appeared to have succeeded because of the promotion of policy debate, improving trust between and among stakeholders, clarity of role definition and the management of the political and administrative interface which strengthened the co-ordinating relationship in the policy development and management process. An innovation in the Zambian model is the publication of the Cabinet Handbook which informs new ministers and permanent secretaries how government operates, and which delineates the roles, functions and responsibilities of each official.

ZIMBABWE

As will be emphasised in the following sub-section to this chapter, the main agency through which African states – including those of Southern Africa – can hope to confront the historical and economic problems that have also been magnified and compounded by the spectre of globalisation, is regional co-operation and integration, from the sub-regional level to the continental level, as represented by the proposed African Economic Community. In the meantime, the exchange of information and experiences in the field of public service reform and management is already showing commendable results in Southern Africa. Such initiatives as those undertaken through the Commonwealth Secretariat, the Southern African Regional Institute for Policy Studies (SARIPS) of the SAPES Trust AAPAM, and Eastern and Southern African Management Institute (ESAMI) have been important contributions in this regard. Not surprisingly, there has been some relationship between the Southern African Initiative for Development (SAID), an institution influenced by the Malaysian and South East Asian experiences in "smart partnership" between the state, labour and other sectors of the private sector, and key consultative fora being established in such countries as Zimbabwe. These fora should assist the process of linking the state with the broader society as a pre-condition of tackling globalisation while also developing a national consensus and strategy on the economic front.

Recently established in Zimbabwe has been the National Economic Consultative Forum (NECF)[29] whose objectives are:

i. to create a "smart partnership" amongst key economic players, namely: government, private sector, labour and other stakeholders, in order to enhance the economic development process of the nation;

ii. to provide a broad participatory framework in the formation of national economic policy through an interchange of ideas and experiences amongst government, private sector, labour, academia and civil society; and

iii. to facilitate the co-ordination, monitoring and evaluation of national economic policy implementation.

These objectives are based on some aspects of the economic and political context of Zimbabwe which influence policy formulation and management processes. The Government decided to form the National Economic Consultative Forum, having identified some contradictory factors such as:

- the government's commitment to social equity, countered by the failure of economic growth, the fall in disposable income and growing social unrest.

- its ideological propensity to state intervention, countered by an inability to maintain public sector investment and strong pressures to liberalisation under a structural adjustment programme. The Government, often under pressure from donors as well as from internal forces for change, had to rethink its service provision roles as well as its policy development processes. The formation of the Forum constitutes an important component of the changing practice of public sector management in Zimbabwe.

The whole issue of smart partnership is based on the principle that any economy is an integral whole with the general infrastructure, businesses process and social responsibilities all feeding one into the other. It is about creating limitless opportunities and wealth that is shared, sustainable and that allows the participants to function in the global economy. Its successful functioning depends on a win-win and prosper-the-neighbour relationship among partners. All the partners, whether they be political leaders, civil servants, entrepreneurs, corporate leaders, management, labour, academia and civic society in general, play different roles according to their different circumstances, but all operating from the same set of principles.

The National Economic Consultative Process, therefore, has embraced the principles of smart partnership such that it forms the local interface with similar regional and international initiatives. It facilitates a fast-track relationship between policy (state), business, labour, academia and civil society. This ensures the effectiveness and timeliness of implementation of national development policies and programmes as agreed by government and all stakeholders through a direct co-ordinated process involving regular consultation, feedback, accountability and contribution by all, and amongst key players, on a mutual win-win, cross-fertilisation relationship.

The structural framework for the Forum was worked out by the Steering Committee of the Forum which was made up of senior government officials, private sector, labour, civic society and academia. This steering committee, which was chaired by the Office of the President and Cabinet, held thirty-two meetings prior to the establishment of the NECF and the First Retreat of the NECF held on the 22 January, 1998 was attended by over five hundred participants from all sectors of the economy. The President has attended and participated in two of the three Executive Core Group Meetings of the Forum and two retreats.

The Forum itself is made up of a hundred and eighty individuals who have been chosen on the basis of their contribution to the national economy broadly representing Government, private sector, labour, academia and civic society. It has to be pointed out that labour has been involved in the establishment of the consultative process since its inception. Up to this point, the slot for labour is still available should the Zimbabwe Congress of Trade Unions (ZCTU) decide to join the consultative process.

The national consultative process does not seek to replace the usual consultation process that takes place between line ministries and their different constituencies, e.g. the tripartite consultations between the Ministry of Public Service, Labour and Social Welfare; the ZCTU and Employers Confederation of Zimbabwe (EMCOZ); Ministry of Lands and Agriculture with farming organisations; Ministry of Industry and Commerce with the Chamber of Zimbabwe Industries (CZI); Zimbabwe National Chamber of Commerce (ZNCC); and the Consumer Council. The Forum deals with issues on a national basis rather than on a sectoral basis.

The Executive Core Group, which has already been selected, except for the labour representation, is made up of forty members. It is the Executive Arm of the Forum and is assisted by a Nucleus Think Tank to research into issues that come up from time to time from the deliberations of the NECF.

The Nucleus Research Think Tank, which has also been appointed, comprises experts in various fields who will undertake research on specific topics and come up with recommendations on the way forward. Each of the topics researched should result in various policy options and their likely impact on the economy. The Nucleus Research Think Tank will co-opt other researchers as the need arises and will report to the chairpersons of the task forces, who in turn will report to the co-chairpersons of the Executive Core Group.

The Secretariat, to be headed by an Executive Secretary, will carry out the day-to-day activities of the Forum and co-ordinate the various task forces and committees that will be set up from time to time.

The initial funding of the activities of the National Economic Consultative Forum will come from donors for two years while mechanisms are being worked out for it to be self-sustaining. It is envisaged that the activities of the Forum will be financed through contributions from the private sector, labour unions and from a regular budget from government. The Forum will also carry out various fund-raising activities such as workshops, seminars, publications etc.

The Executive Core Group has so far held three meetings. The first meeting discussed the stabilisation of food prices, whose recommendations assisted the work of the Ministerial Task Force on the stabilisation of food prices. The second meeting discussed plans on the way forward for the Forum, especially the formation of task forces to deal with issues of immediate concern to the nation. The third meeting appointed task forces and also discussed the problem of unemployment and strategies to tackle the problem.

The task forces that have been formed are to deal with the immediate issues of concern to the nation. The following task forces have been set up:

- Incomes and Pricing Policy task force;
- Macro-economic Policy task force;
- Industrial Policy task force;
- Indigenisation task force; and
- National Land Reform Programme task force.

These task forces comprise members of the Executive Core Group and will utilise the Research Think Tank for research into various issues. It should be noted that the task forces are not permanent. After completing their tasks, they will be replaced by other task forces. All the work programmes will be time-framed with specific deadlines set, and projects are to be completed as per the agreed recommendations and time-frame. The emphasis will be on practical solutions to deal with pressing issues that are facing the country.

It is expected that the NECF will also interface with regional and international initiatives of the "Smart Partnership" such as the Langkawi International Dialogue and the Southern African International Dialogue. The NECF will also be a vehicle for the promotion of investment programmes locally and overseas.

TOWARDS REGIONAL POLICY CO-ORDINATION AND COLLABORATION

The Zimbabwe model outlined above is a demonstration of the benefits that flow from attempts to integrate into national situations some of the latest innovations, in policy analysis, co-ordination and collaboration, from specific global and sub-regional experiences in the field. The idea of smart partnership is one such, drawn as it is, through the Commonwealth context, from Malaysia and designed into the regional one that is the Southern African Investment Dialogue (SAID) out of which the "Zimbabwe model" has developed and promises to be so crucial in the process of national economic and political recovery. Therefore, the importance of such workshops as constitute the subject of this work cannot be exaggerated and these initiatives will have to be pursued carefully through closer working relationships between the Commonwealth Secretariat and other continental and sub-regional institutions as AAPAM and SARIPS/SAPES Trust. In this way, "models" drawn from global and specifically Commonwealth, sub-regional and national contexts can be extolled, elaborated and developed into viable interventions in the study of policy analysis and management affairs. Besides, the inherent values of regional and continental blocs no longer require spirited justification; in the era of globalisation, Africa – and its sub-regional blocs – can only survive and become a factor in global affairs through unity of purpose.

However, even the field of policy analysis and public service management will have to take cognisance of the current constraints and limitations to regional co-operation and integration in Africa. This is necessary also because the field itself will have to develop and establish strategies through which to counteract these historically-based problems and thereby contribute directly to the promotion of the African Economic Community, beginning with the various sub-regional blocs that are currently in the form of the Southern African Development Community (SADC); East African Co-operation (EAC); Economic Community of West African States (ECOWAS); Community of Eastern and Southern Africa (COMESA) etc.

The constraints to regional co-operation and integration in Africa are broadly three-fold and are inter-related. First, the problem of vertical integration into the northern hemisphere. As explained at the beginning of this chapter, this is the historical and colonial legacy: it continues to undermine co-operative, co-ordinating and collaborating efforts among member states of Africa *vis a vis* the northern hemisphere in general and globalisation in particular. The problems associated with this express themselves in the endless competition among African states for aid, access to markets and even preferential treatment. This creates a "hierarchy of powers" at both the continental and sub-regional levels, undermining co-ordination and collaboration at the various levels of inter-state and inter-institutional processes. Second, the problem of uneven and unequal development within and between the African countries themselves, not to mention that between the sub-regional blocs in the making. Among many other things, this gives rise to the problem of reconciling competing interests among member states, and of joint mobilisation of resources for programme development.

Third, the problem of the development of nation-state-in-the-making. Reference has already been made to this at the beginning of this chapter. The point is that unstable and insecure states are inimical not only to the enterprise of regional co-operation and integration but also to the processes of policy co-ordination and collaboration.

REFERENCES

1. Plowden, W., *Ministers and Mandarins Institute for Public Policy Research*, London 1994, p 153.

2. Kaul, M., *Better Policy Support: Improving Policy Management in the Public Service*. Managing the Public Service: Strategies for Improvement Series No. 4. Commonwealth Secretariat 1997.

3. UNDP, Public Sector Management, Governance and Sustainable Development, Box 5, pp 56–57, unpublished report.

4. Recardo Petrella as quoted in Panchamukhi, V. R., *Globalisation Competition and Economic Stability Paradigm*, Vol. I No. 2, January 1998.

5. Panchamukhi V. R. op cit.

6. Ibbo Mandaza (ed) "Introduction", *Peace and Security in Southern Africa*, SAPES Books, 1996.

7. Westergaard, J. H., Sociology: The Myth of Classes in Blackburn, R. *Ideology in Social Science* Fontana, New York, 1972, p 121.

8. Navarro, V., *Medicine under Capitalism*, Prodist. New York, 1977, p 209.

9. Offe, C. The Theory of the Capitalist State and the Problem of Policy Formulation. In Lindberg, H., et al (eds) *Stress and Contradiction in Modern Capitalism*, Lexington Books, London 1975, p 126.

10. Navarro, V., op cit p 212.

11. Navarro, ibid p 217.

12. Andrew Korac-Kakabadse & Kada Korac-Kakabadse, *Leadership in Government: Study of the Australian Public Service*. Ashgate Publishing Ltd, Aldershot, Hants, 1998, pp 108.

13. Corkery, J., and Land, A., *Public Service Reforms*, European Centre for Development Policy Management, Maastricht (ECDPM) No. 7 September 1997.

14. The Role of Government in Adjusting Economies, Paper 2: Implications and Impact of Structural Adjustment on the Civil Service: The Case of Ghana: Development Administration Group, School of Public Policy, the University of Birmingham, by George Larbi, October 1995.

15. (a) **Malawi**
    Public Service Act, May 1996
    Action Plan for Civil Service Reform, September 1996

    (b) **Botswana**
    Strategic Management for Improved Performance Seminar: Report: 12–13 June 1995 at Mowani Safari Lodge, Kasane

    (c) **Swaziland**
    Economic and Social Reform Agenda (ESRA), 10 December 1996

    (d) **Zambia**
    Public Service Reform Programme (PSRP), November 1993

    (e) **Zimbabwe:**
    A Framework for Economic Reform (1991–95)

16. Cauifield, Catherine: *The World Bank and the Poverty of Nations*: Masters of Illusion: Macmillan Publishers Ltd, London 1997.

17. Report of the *Regional Workshop for Senior Policy Managers in Sub-Saharan Africa*, prepared by the Development Policy Management Forum (DPMF), May 1997.

18. Corkery, J., Land, A., Bossuyt, J., *The Process of Policy Formulation: Institutional Path or Institutional Maze?* Policy Management Report No 3. European Centre for Development Policy Management. December 1995, p 1.

19. Jorm, N., Hunt, J., Manning, N., *Working Towards Results: Managing Individual Performance in the Public Service.* Managing the Public Service: Strategies for Improvement Series: No 3. Commonwealth Secretariat 1996 p 1.

20. Herald, Harare, 5 May 1997.

21. Southern African Regional Institute for Policy Studies Masters in Policy Studies: Research, Dialogue, Policy Studies: Research, Dialogues Policy SARIPS Prospectus 1995 – 1996. Sapes Trust 1995. p 1.

22. Times, Thursday, 8 May 1997.

23. Hunn, D.K, *Measuring Performance in Policy Advice A New Zealand Perspective* in Public Management Occasional Papers 1994 No 5. Performance Measurement in Government Issues and Illustration OCDE Organisation for Economic Co-operation and Development, Paris 1994 p 29.

24. Healey, J. and Robinson, M., *Democracy, Governance and Economic Policy*. ODI, London 1992.

25. PUMA Policy Brief No. 5, Public Management Service, May 1998, OECD.

26. Chakalisa, M, Policy Development in Botswana. An unpublished paper presented at the Harare Regional Policy Analysis Seminar, September 1997.

27. Julie Koenen-Grant, Harry Garnett: Improving Policy Formulation and Implementation in Zambia, August 1995. Unpublished paper by Abt Associates of USA.

28. ibid

29. Zimbabwe National Economic Consultative Forum, Office of the President and Cabinet (June 1998).